ECCE ROMANI

A Latin Reading Course
Prepared by The Scottish Classics Group

2
Rome at Last

Second Edition

Oliver & Boyd

Illustrated by Trevor Parkin and Tom Reid
Cover illustration by Peter Dennis

Oliver & Boyd
Robert Stevenson House
1–3 Baxter's Place
Leith Walk
Edinburgh EH1 3BB
A Division of Longman Group Limited

First published 1971
Second edition 1982
Fourth impression 1985

ISBN 0 05 003466 9

Set in 11/12 and 10/12pt Baskerville
Produced by Longman Group (FE) Ltd
Printed in Hong Kong

Contents

17
Arrival at the Inn

raeda in fossa haerebat. Cornelii per viam ibant ad cauponam quae non procul aberat. Cornelia, quae non iam lacrimabat, cum Eucleide ambulabat. pueros, quod praecurrebant, identidem revocabat Cornelius. Aurelia, quamquam in caupona pernoctare adhuc nolebat, lente cum Cornelio ibat.

mox ad cauponam appropinquabant. neminem videbant; voces tamen hominum audiebant.

subito duo canes ex ianua cauponae se praecipitant et ferociter latrantes Cornelios petunt. statim fugit Sextus. stat immobilis Marcus. Aurelia perterrita exclamat. Cornelius ipse nihil facit. Cornelia tamen non fugit sed ad canes manum extendit.

"ecce, Marce!" inquit. "hi canes latrant modo. nullum est periculum. ecce, Sexte! caudam movent."

eo ipso tempore ad ianuam cauponae apparuit homo obesus qui canes revocavit.

"salvete, hospites!" inquit. "in caupona mea pernoctare vultis? hic multi cives praeclari pernoctaverunt. olim hic pernoctavit etiam legatus principis."

"salve, mi Apollodore!" interpellavit Eucleides. "quid agis?"

"mehercule!" respondit caupo. "nisi erro, meum amicum Eucleidem video."

"non erras" inquit Eucleides. "laetus te video. quod raeda domini mei in fossa haeret immobilis, necesse est hic in caupona pernoctare."

"doleo" inquit caupo "quod raeda est in fossa, sed gaudeo quod ad meam cauponam nunc venitis. intrate, intrate, omnes!"

praecurro, praecurrere (3), to run ahead
homo, hominis (*m*), man
se praecipitant, (they) hurl themselves
fugio, fugere (3), to flee
manus, hand
hi canes, these dogs
modo, only
cauda, -ae (*f*), tail
apparuit, (he) appeared
obesus, -a, -um, fat
revocavit, (he) called back

hospes, hospitis (*m*), friend, guest
pernoctaverunt, (they) have spent the night
olim, once (upon a time)
legatus, -i (*m*), envoy
quid agis? How are you?
mehercule! by Hercules! Goodness me!
nisi erro, unless I am mistaken
doleo, dolere (2), to be sad

Exercise 17a

Using story 17 as a guide, translate into Latin:

1 The inn was not far away.
2 Cornelius kept calling the boys back.
3 Aurelia did not want to spend the night in the inn.
4 Two dogs are making for the boys.
5 The two dogs are wagging their tails.
6 I am glad to see you.
7 The innkeeper is sorry that the coach is in the ditch.

cave canem!   *Beware of the dog!*
humanum est errare.   *To err is human.*

REGULAR VERBS

Most Latin verbs belong to one or other of four groups:

Present Tense

		Group 1	Group 2	Group 3	Group 4
Singular	1	par**o**	habe**o**	mitt**o**	audi**o**
	2	para**s**	habe**s**	mitti**s**	audi**s**
	3	para**t**	habe**t**	mitti**t**	audi**t**
Plural	1	para**mus**	habe**mus**	mitti**mus**	audi**mus**
	2	para**tis**	habe**tis**	mitti**tis**	audi**tis**
	3	para**nt**	habe**nt**	mittu**nt**	audiu**nt**
Infinitive		par**are**	hab**ere**	mitt**ere**	aud**ire**
Imperative		par**a**	habe	mitt**e**	audi
		par**ate**	hab**ete**	mitt**ite**	aud**ite**

Imperfect Tense

		Group 1	Group 2	Group 3	Group 4
Singular	1	para**bam**	habe**bam**	mitte**bam**	audie**bam**
	2	para**bas**	habe**bas**	mitte**bas**	audie**bas**
	3	para**bat**	habe**bat**	mitte**bat**	audie**bat**
Plural	1	para**bamus**	habe**bamus**	mitte**bamus**	audie**bamus**
	2	para**batis**	habe**batis**	mitte**batis**	audie**batis**
	3	para**bant**	habe**bant**	mitte**bant**	audie**bant**

IRREGULAR VERBS

A few verbs do not belong to any of the four groups shown on the previous page, e.g. **sum** (I am) and **volo** (I want), but you will notice that, except for the forms **sum** and **possum**, they have the same *person* endings as the regular verbs.

Present Tense

Singular	1	su**m**	possu**m**	e**o**	vol**o**	nol**o**
	2	e**s**	pote**s**	i**s**	vi**s**	non vi**s**
	3	es**t**	potest	i**t**	vul**t**	non vul**t**
Plural	1	su**mus**	possu**mus**	i**mus**	volu**mus**	nolu**mus**
	2	es**tis**	potes**tis**	i**tis**	vul**tis**	non vul**tis**
	3	su**nt**	possu**nt**	eu**nt**	volu**nt**	nolu**nt**
Infinitive		esse	posse	ire	velle	nolle
Impera-tive		es	—	i	—	noli
		este	—	ite	—	nolite

Imperfect Tense

Singular	1	era**m**	potera**m**	i**bam**	vole**bam**	nole**bam**
	2	era**s**	potera**s**	i**bas**	vole**bas**	nole**bas**
	3	era**t**	potera**t**	i**bat**	vole**bat**	nole**bat**
Plural	1	era**mus**	potera**mus**	i**bamus**	vole**bamus**	nole**bamus**
	2	era**tis**	potera**tis**	i**batis**	vole**batis**	nole**batis**
	3	era**nt**	potera**nt**	i**bant**	vole**bant**	nole**bant**

Exercise 17b

Translate the following short sentences, paying particular attention to the tense of the verb:

1 ubi manebat?
2 unde veniunt?
   unde? where ... from?
3 cur ire non poterant?
4 quid faciebatis?
5 quo ire volunt?
6 quid respondebant?
7 cur praecurrebant?
8 quid facere eum iubebat?
9 quid ridebatis?
10 quid ferebas?
11 quid facitis?
12 quid vides?
13 ubi haeret raeda?
14 quo ibant?
15 unde veniebas?
16 quo equos ducit?
17 quo fugiebant?
18 cur ire nolunt?
19 caupona non procul aberat.
20 manere nolebamus.

ADJECTIVES

Latin adjectives fall into two main categories – Group 1/2 and Group 3:

		Group 1/2			Group 3		
		Masc.	Fem.	Neut.	Masc.	Fem.	Neut.
S.	Nom.	magnus	magna	magnum	omnis	omnis	omne
	Acc.	magnum	magnam	magnum	omnem	omnem	omne
	Gen.	magni	magnae	magni	omnis	omnis	omnis
	Abl.	magno	magna	magno	omni	omni	omni
P.	Nom.	magni	magnae	magna	omnes	omnes	omnia
	Acc.	magnos	magnas	magna	omnes	omnes	omnia
	Gen.	magnorum	magnarum	magnorum	omnium	omnium	omnium
	Abl.	magnis	magnis	magnis	omnibus	omnibus	omnibus

N.B. Some adjectives of Group 1/2 end in **-r** in the masculine nominative singular, e.g. **noster, nostra, nostrum; miser, misera, miserum.**

AGREEMENT OF ADJECTIVES

The ending of an adjective is determined by the noun with which it *agrees*. For example, in the sentence

multos agros, multas arbores, multa plaustra vident.

since **agros** is a masculine noun in the accusative plural, **multos** has a masculine accusative plural ending.

Similarly, **multas** is feminine accusative plural *agreeing* with **arbores,** and **multa** is neuter accusative plural *agreeing* with **plaustra**.

There are five clues which help you to decide with which noun an adjective agrees. These are *sense, position, number, gender* and *case.*

1 *Let us look at the last three clues (agreement):*

(*a*) Sometimes any one of the three *agreement* clues will give you the right answer:

mater bonos pueros laudat.
The mother praises the good boys.

mater and **pueros** are different in gender, number and case, and therefore all the clues in **bonos** are decisive.

(*b*) Sometimes only two of these clues are present:

mater bonas puellas laudat.
The mother praises the good girls.

In this sentence **mater** and **puellas** have the same gender, but either of the two other clues (number and case) will help.

(*c*) In the following sentences only one of the *agreement* clues is present:

mater bonam puellam laudat.
The mother praises the good girl.

Since **mater** and **puellam** have the same gender and number, only the case of **bonam** is decisive.

matrem bonum puerum laudare iubemus.
We order the mother to praise the good boy.

Here, it is the gender alone which is decisive.

matrem bonas puellas laudare iubemus.
We order the mother to praise the good girls.

Here, only the number is decisive.

2 *You will find examples where none of the clues of agreement will help you. When this happens, you must rely on position or sense:*

puellam ignavam epistolam scribere iubemus.
We order the lazy girl to write the letter.

Exercise 17c

In the following sentences the most important clues to meaning are those of agreement of adjectives. Sometimes, especially in poetry, words appear in an unusual order.

Translate:

1 canis magnus ossa habet.   **os, ossis** (*n*), bone
2 canis magna ossa habet.
3 multi canes ossa habent.
4 canis magnum os habet.
5 multa ossa magnus canis habet.
6 magna habent multi canes ossa.
7 magnum canis habet os.
8 multi canes dominos non habent.
9 magnum habet dominus canem.
10 canem dominus magnum habet.
11 habent multi pueri magnos canes.
12 magnos multi habent pueri canes.

18
Settling in

cunti in cauponam intraverunt.

"nonne cenare vultis?" inquit caupo. "servi mei bonam cenam vobis statim parare possunt."

"ego et Cornelia" inquit Aurelia "hic cenare non possumus. duc nos statim ad cubiculum nostrum."

servos caupo statim iussit cenam Cornelio et Marco et Sexto parare. ipse Aureliam et Corneliam ad cubiculum duxit. Aurelia, ubi lectum vidit, gemuit.

"hic lectus est sordidus" inquit. "mea Cornelia in sordido lecto dormire non potest. necesse est alium lectum in cubiculum movere."

caupo respondit "cur me reprehendis? multi viatores ad meam cauponam venire solent. nemo meam cauponam reprehendit."

iam advenit Eucleides. ubi Aurelia rem explicavit, Eucleides quoque cauponem reprehendit.

caupo mussavit. "prope viam Appiam cauponam meliorem invenire non potestis. in caupona mea nulli lecti sunt sordidi."

sed servos iussit alium lectum petere. brevi tempore servi alium lectum in cubiculum portaverunt. caupo iam cum risu clamavit "ecce, domina! servi mei alium lectum tibi paraverunt. nonne nunc cenare vultis?"

"ego non iam esurio" inquit Cornelia. "volo tantum cubitum ire."

"ego quoque" inquit Aurelia "sum valde defessa."

non cenaverunt Aurelia et Cornelia, sed cubitum statim iverunt. mox dormiebant.

intraverunt, (they) entered	**Cornelio,** for Cornelius
ceno, cenare (1), to dine	**duxit,** (he) led
cena, -ae (*f*), dinner	**lectus, -i** (*m*), bed
vobis, for you	**hic lectus,** this bed
duc! take! lead! (imperative)	**sordidus, -a, -um,** dirty
iussit, (he) ordered	**viator, viatoris** (*m*), traveller

venire solent, (they) are in the habit of coming
rem explicare, to explain the situation
melior, better
tibi, for you

esurio, esurire (4), to be hungry
cubitum ire, to go to bed
valde, very, exceedingly
iverunt, they went

VERBS: Perfect Tense

Compare the following pairs of sentences:

servus **mussat.**	*The slave **mutters.***
caupo **mussavit.**	*The innkeeper **muttered.***
Marcus **gemit.**	*Marcus **groans.***
Aurelia **gemuit.**	*Aurelia **groaned.***
Davus servos **iubet** canes ducere.	*Davus **orders** the slaves to bring the dogs.*
caupo servos **iussit** cenam parare.	*The innkeeper **ordered** the slaves to prepare dinner.*
Marcus nuntium in atrium **ducit.**	*Marcus **leads** the messenger into the atrium.*
Corneliam ad cubiculum **duxit.**	*He **led** Cornelia to the bedroom.*

In each of the pairs of examples listed above, the verb in the first example is in the present tense and the verb in the second example is in the *perfect tense.*

The perfect tense refers, not to something that *is happening,* but to something that *happened* or *has happened* in the past.

In the perfect tense the ending of the 3rd person singular is **-it**; the ending of the 3rd person plural is **-erunt**.

In many perfect tenses, the **stem** ends in

> **-v-** or **-u-** or **-s-** or **-x-**

e.g. explica**v**it   gem**u**it   ius**s**it   du**x**it

The perfect endings are added to the perfect stem.

13

Here are some more examples:

SINGULAR		PLURAL	
Present	*Perfect*	*Present*	*Perfect*
exclamat	exclamavit	exclamant	exclamaverunt
audit	audivit	audiunt	audiverunt
habet	habuit	habent	habuerunt
ridet	risit	rident	riserunt
conspicit	conspexit	conspiciunt	conspexerunt

Exercise 18a

Continue as above, completing the blanks:

revocat	_____	_____	revocaverunt
_____	gemuit	gemunt	_____
iubet	iussit	_____	_____
_____	_____	custodiunt	custodiverunt
timet	timuit	_____	_____
_____	traxit	trahunt	_____
_____	_____	_____	mussaverunt
ducit	_____	ducunt	_____

Exercise 18b (Revision)

Cornelii per viam ad cauponam lente ambulabant.

Sextus "nonne ille tabellarius equos vehementer incitavit, Marce?"

cui respondit Marcus "ita vero! eos ferociter verberavit. equi cisium celeriter traxerunt. raedarius noster 'cave, sceleste!' magna voce exclamavit. tum raedam devertebat, sed frustra. tabellarius tamen neque cisium devertit neque raedam vitavit. itaque equi raedam in fossam traxerunt. gemuit raedarius; gemuerunt pater et mater; lacrimavit Cornelia."

"pater tuus certe iratus erat" interpellavit Sextus. "statim virgam arripuit et miserum raedarium verberabat. Cornelia, ubi hoc vidit, iterum lacrimavit. 'pater! pater!' inquit. 'noli miserum hominem verberare!'"

"tum pater" inquit Marcus "Corneliam tacere iussit. omnes
solliciti caelum spectaverunt quod iam advesperascebat. pater
igitur Eucleidem nos ad cauponam ducere iussit."

mox cauponam conspexerunt. intraverunt Cornelii et brevi
tempore cenaverunt.

vehementer incitare, to drive hard	**hoc,** this
arripuit, he seized	

Exercise 18c

Using Exercise 18b as a guide, translate into Latin:
1 The driver shouted "Watch out!"
2 The courier did not avoid the coach.
3 Cornelia burst out crying.
4 Father and Mother groaned.
5 The coachman groaned.
6 Father ordered Cornelia to be quiet.
7 The horses dragged the carriage into the ditch.
8 In a short time the Cornelii had dinner.

Exercise 18d (Revision)

dum Cornelii ad cauponam lente ibant, raedarius equos
custodiebat. miser erat quod Cornelium timebat. mox adven-
iunt duo servi cauponis.

"salve!" inquiunt. "quid accidit? quid faciebas? raedamne
ferociter agebas? cur non diligenter viam spectabas?
dormiebasne?"

sed raedarius miser "minime vero!" respondet. "raedam
magna arte agebam. pueri me vexabant; tacere nolebant. ego
certe non dormiebam. sed cur vos adestis? vultisne me adiuvare?
potestisne raedam ex fossa extrahere?"

tum omnes diu laborabant, sed raedam neque servi neque
equi extrahere poterant. tandem defessi ad cauponam redeunt.

"raedam movere non poteramus" inquiunt. "necesse est
magnum numerum servorum mittere."

accidit, (it) happened	**adiuvare,** to help
diligenter, carefully	

Horace's Journey

This account of Horace's journey from Rome to Brundisium describes some of the hazards with which travellers might be faced:

After I had left great Rome, I put up in Aricia in a humble inn. My companion was Heliodorus, a teacher of rhetoric. From there we went to Forum Appii, a town packed with boatmen and grasping innkeepers. We were idle enough to take this part of the journey in two stages; for the more energetic it is only one; the Appian Way is less tiring for leisurely travellers. Here, because of the water, which is very bad, I suffered an upset stomach; and it was in a bad temper that I waited for my companions to finish their evening meal. As we were about to go on board, the boatmen began to argue. A whole hour went past while the fares were being collected and the mule harnessed. The vicious mosquitoes and marsh-frogs made sleep impossible while the boatman, who had drunk too much cheap wine, sang of his absent girl-friend, and a passenger joined in the singing. At last the

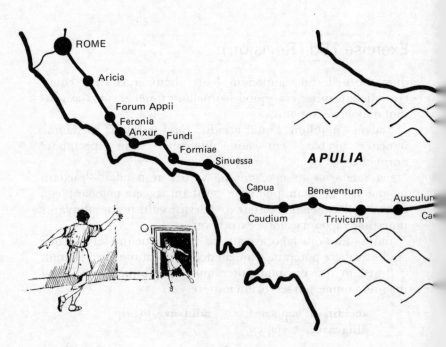

weary passengers fell asleep; and the idle boatman turned the mule out to graze, fastened its halter to a stone and lay on his back snoring.

At dawn we realised we weren't moving. A hot-tempered passenger leapt up and beat boatman and mule with a stick. When at last we disembarked, it was almost ten o'clock. With due reverence and ceremony we washed our hands and faces in the fountain of Feronia. After lunch we "crawled" the five kilometres to Anxur, which is perched on rocks that shine white in the distance. There our very good friend Maecenas was due to meet us. As my eyes were giving me trouble, I smeared black ointment on them. Meanwhile Maecenas arrived with that perfect gentleman, Fonteius Capito. We were glad to leave Fundi behind, with its self-appointed "praetor" Aufidius Luscus. How we laughed at the official get-up of the ambition-crazy clerk, his toga praetexta and the tunic with the broad stripe. At last, tired out, we stayed in the city of Formiae, where Murena provided accommodation and Capito a meal.

The next day we reached Sinuessa and were met by Varius, Plotius and Vergil—friends to whom I was most attached. Then a small villa next to the Campanian bridge gave us shelter; and

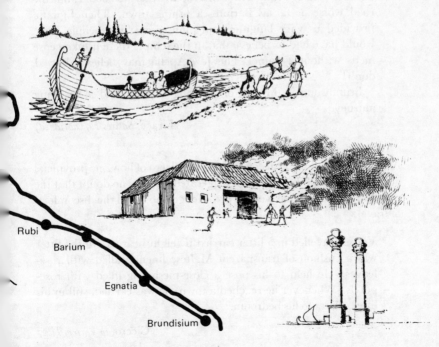

Rubi

Barium

Egnatia

Brundisium

17

the official purveyors, as they were obliged to do, provided us with wood and salt. After we left here, our pack-mules were unsaddled early at Capua. Maecenas went to play ball, Vergil and I to sleep; for ball-games are bad for a man with sore eyes and an upset stomach. After Capua, Cocceius received us in a well-stored house built above the inns of Caudium.

From here we made our way right on to Beneventum, where the overworked innkeeper nearly burned the place down while roasting lean thrushes on a spit. Soon after leaving Beneventum, I saw again the familiar mountains of my native Apulia. We would never have struggled over those mountains, if we had not found lodgings at Trivicum. There the smoke made our eyes water, for they put green branches on the fire, leaves and all.

From here we sped on thirty-eight kilometres in carriages, intending to lodge in the small town of Ausculum. Here they charge for the cheapest of all commodities—water. The bread, however, is very good indeed, so that the experienced traveller usually takes some away in his bag; for the bread at Canusium is as hard as a stone, and the water supply is no better.

From here we arrived at Rubi, tired out—as was to be expected—for the stage was long and the road conditions difficult because of heavy rain. After this the weather was better, but the road worse as far as Barium, a fishing town. Then Egnatia provided us with laughter and amusement; the people there would have had us believe that in the temple there frankincense melts without a flame. The Jew Apella may believe that—I don't!

Brundisium is the end of my long account and of my long journey.

Horace, *Satires I.5 (abridged)*

Although the following account given by Cicero of how one provincial governor travelled is probably exaggerated, there is no doubt that the rich and powerful often went to great lengths to avoid the discomforts of travel:

Verres travelled in a litter carried by eight bearers. In the litter was a cushion of transparent Maltese linens stuffed with rose-leaves. He held to his nose a close-mesh bag filled with rose-petals. Whenever he reached a town, he was carried, still in his litter, direct to his bedroom.

Cicero, *in Verrem II.27*

Travel by Land

Gaius Cornelius and his family travelled from Baiae to Rome along a section of the Via Appia, which ran south from Rome to Brundisium—a distance of 576 kilometres. It was part of the network of major highways that radiated from the Golden Milestone (**miliarium aureum**), in the Forum at Rome, to all parts of the Empire. These roads, originally built by the legions to make easy movement of troops possible, were laid on carefully-made foundations with drainage channels at both sides, and were usually paved with slabs of basalt. Although travel was safer and easier than at any time before the "Railway Age", it was nevertheless extremely slow by modern standards. The **raeda** seldom averaged more than eight kilometres per hour; a man walking might manage forty kilometres a day; an imperial courier on urgent business might, with frequent changes of horse, manage to cover over 240 kilometres in twenty-four hours. Since carriage wheels had iron rims and vehicles lacked springs, a journey by road was bound to be uncomfortable. Moreover, since the vehicles were open or, at best, had only a canopy, the travellers often had to endure both clouds of dust and attacks from insects.

The following passage illustrates these discomforts:

> When I had to make my way back from Baiae to Naples, to avoid the experience of sailing a second time, I easily convinced myself that a storm was raging. The whole road was so deep in mud that I might as well have gone by sea. That day I had to endure what athletes put up with as a matter of course: after being anointed with mud, we were dusted with sand in the Naples tunnel. Nothing could be longer than that prison-like corridor, nothing dimmer than those torches that do not dispel the darkness but merely make us more aware of it. But even if there were light there, it would be blacked out by the dust which, however troublesome and disagreeable it may be in the open, is, as you can imagine, a thousand times worse in an enclosed space where there is no ventilation and the dust rises in one's face. These were the two entirely different discomforts which we suffered. On the same day and on the same road we struggled through both mud and dust.
>
> Seneca, *Epistolae Morales 57*

19
Chance Encounter

ubi Cornelia et mater cubitum iverunt, Marcus et Sextus cum
Cornelio manserunt. cum Cornelio cenare et post cenam ad
mediam noctem vigilare in animo habuerunt, nam omnia
videre et omnia audire voluerunt.

Marcus "esurio, pater" inquit. "esurisne tu quoque, Sexte?"
"ita vero!" respondit Sextus.

"semper esuritis, tu et Marcus" exclamavit Cornelius.

"licetne nobis" inquit Marcus "hic cenare?"

paulisper tacebat pater, sed tandem "esto!" inquit. "tibi et
Sexto licet hic cenare. post cenam tamen necesse est statim
cubitum ire."

riserunt pueri quod laeti erant. "gaudemus, pater" inquit
Marcus "quod nos in cubiculum non statim misisti. voluimus
enim hic manere et alios viatores spectare."

tum Cornelius cauponem iussit cibum parare. brevi tempore
servus cibum ad eos portavit. dum pueri cibum devorant,
subito intravit miles quidam. Cornelium attente spectavit.
"salve, vir optime!" inquit. "salvete, pueri! cur vos in hanc
cauponam intravistis? cur non ad villam hospitis ivistis? nonne
tu es senator Romanus?"

"senator Romanus sum" respondit Cornelius. "nos in hanc
cauponam intravimus quod raeda nostra in fossa haeret
immobilis. in agris nocte manere nolebamus, sed numquam
antea in caupona pernoctavimus. certe in agris pernoctare est
periculosum."

tum miles "etiam in caupona pernoctare saepe est
periculosum."

"cur hoc nobis dicis?" rogavit Cornelius. "estne hic caupo
homo scelestus? de Apollodoro quid audivisti?"

"de Apollodoro nihil audivi, sed semper est periculosum in
caupona pernoctare. vosne audivistis illam fabulam de caupone
narratam? ille caupo hospitem necavit."

"minime!" inquit Cornelius. "illam fabulam non audivi. cur
igitur nobis illam non narras dum cenamus?"

manserunt, (they) stayed
post (+ *acc.*), after
media nox, midnight
vigilo, vigilare (1), to stay
  awake
in animo habere, to intend
licet nobis, we are allowed
paulisper, for a short time
esto! all right!
misisti, you have sent
voluimus, we wanted
enim, for
miles quidam, a soldier
miles, militis (*m*), soldier
vir optime! sir!

in hanc cauponam, into this
  inn
nocte, at night
numquam, never
antea, before
dico, dicere (3), to say
de (+ *abl.*), about
audivi, I have heard
**illam fabulam de caupone
narratam,** that famous
  story about the innkeeper
neco, necare (1), to kill
narro, narrare (1), to tell (a
  story)

VERBS: Perfect Tense

You have now met all the endings of the perfect tense.

Singular	1	**-i**	Plural	1	**-imus**
	2	**-isti**		2	**-istis**
	3	**-it**		3	**-erunt**

These are the endings of the perfect tense of *all* Latin verbs, e.g.

Singular	1	mis**i**	Plural	1	mis**imus**
	2	mis**isti**		2	mis**istis**
	3	mis**it**		3	mis**erunt**

Exercise 19a

Using story 19 as a guide, translate into Latin:
1 Cornelius ordered the innkeeper to prepare food.
2 Suddenly a soldier entered.
3 Why did you come into this inn?

4 We have never before spent a night in an inn.
5 What have you heard about Apollodorus?
6 I haven't heard that story.

Exercise 19b

Translate:

1 Marcus et Sextus ad mediam noctem vigilare in animo
   habuerunt.
2 ego et tu cubitum ire noluimus.
3 milesne Cornelium spectavit?
4 cur voluisti hic pernoctare, Marce?
5 cur in caupona pernoctavistis, pueri? licetne filio senatoris in
   cauponam intrare?
6 Cornelius in cubiculum servum ire iussit.
7 pueri laeti fuerunt quod ad mediam noctem vigilaverunt.
8 dum Cornelius et pueri cenant, miles fabulam narravit.
9 ego et Cornelius in agris manere timebamus.
10 omnia videre, audire, narrare volunt quod numquam antea in
   caupona pernoctaverunt.

fui, I was (perfect of **sum**)

Exercise 19c

Translate:

1 ego liberos in horto petivi; tu eos in silvis invenisti.
2 ubi tunica Sexti in ramis haerebat, nos omnes risimus.
3 quo ivisti, Cornelia? ego et Marcus patrem hoc rogavimus, sed
   ille nihil respondit.
4 quamquam Sextus fuit molestus, servi eum non verberaverunt.
5 ubi heri fuistis, Marce et Cornelia? pater et mater nos iusserunt
   hic manere.
6 postquam cenavimus, cubitum ire voluimus.
7 heri ad urbem ivimus, sed matrem ibi non vidimus.
8 "unde venistis, amici?" rogavit caupo. "quo nunc itis?"
9 tune Cornelium vidisti, ubi Romam advenisti? ego certe eum non
   vidi.
10 ille, postquam hoc audivit, ex caupona se praecipitavit.

ille, he   **postquam,** after
heri, yesterday

Roman Hospitality

Because inns were dirty and often dangerous, well-to-do Romans tried to avoid staying in them. Instead they tried to plan their journey so that they could stay at the villa of a **hospes**. This word means a "host" or a "guest", but it is also translated as a "friend", although in this special sense it has no exact equivalent in English. It describes a relationship established between two families in the past and kept up by every succeeding generation. As a result of such a relationship a traveller could go to the house of his "family friend"—whom in some cases he personally might never have met—and claim **hospitium** for the night, producing, if need be, some token such as a coin that had been halved as proof of the link between the two families. Members of the host's family, if they happened to be travelling in a district in which their guest's family owned villas, could claim similar rights of hospitality. It could extend to other situations. For instance, if a Roman had business interests in one of the provinces, someone resident there might look after them for him. In return he might have some service done for him at Rome. Cornelius, you may remember, is responsible for Sextus' education while his father is in Asia.

VERBS: Principal Parts

When we refer to a Latin verb, we normally give the four *Principal Parts* from which all parts of that verb are derived:

> the 1st person singular of the present tense,
> the present infinitive,
> the 1st person singular of the perfect tense,
> the supine.

	Present	*Infinitive*	*Perfect*	*Supine*	*Meaning*
Group 1	paro	parare (1)	paravi	paratum	*to prepare*
Group 2	habeo	habere (2)	habui	habitum	*to have*
Group 3	mitto	mittere (3)	misi	missum	*to send*
	facio	facere (3)	feci	factum	*to make, do*
Group 4	audio	audire (4)	audivi	auditum	*to hear*

Most verbs in Groups 1, 2 and 4 follow the patterns on page 24. There is no set pattern for Group 3 verbs.

In vocabulary lists from now onwards, the verbs in Groups 1, 2 and 4 which follow the set patterns will appear as follows:

clamo (1), to shout
appareo (2), to appear
punio (4), to punish

When they do not follow the pattern, they will be given in full, e.g.

lavo, lavare (1), **lavi, lavatum,** to wash
venio, venire (4), **veni, ventum,** to come

Group 3 verbs will also be given in full, e.g.

duco, ducere (3), **duxi, ductum**, to lead

Exercise 19d

From the parts of the verbs given below deduce in each case the first three Principal Parts:

	1st Sing. Present	Present Infinitive	1st Sing. Perfect
necamus, necavimus	neco	necare (1)	necavi
intrant, intraverunt			
erras, erravisti			
tenes, tenuisti			
mittunt, miserunt			
manemus, mansimus			
iubet, iussit			
discedimus, discessimus			
haeret, haesit			
dormiunt, dormiverunt			
petunt, petiverunt			
custodio, custodivimus			
gemunt, gemuit			

20
Murder

duo amici, Aulus et Septimus, dum iter in Graecia faciunt, ad urbem Megaram venerunt. Aulus in caupona pernoctavit, in villa hospitis Septimus. media nocte, dum Septimus dormit, Aulus in somno ei apparuit et clamavit "age, Septime! fer mihi auxilium! caupo me necare parat."

Septimus, somnio perterritus, statim surrexit et, postquam animum recuperavit, "nihil mali" inquit. "somnium modo fuit."

deinde iterum obdormivit. iterum tamen in somno Aulus suo amico apparuit; iterum Septimo clamavit "ubi ego auxilium petivi, tu non venisti. nemo me adiuvare nunc potest. caupo enim me necavit. postquam hoc fecit, corpus meum in plaustro posuit et stercus supra coniecit. in animo habet plaustrum ex urbe cras movere. necesse est igitur cras mane plaustrum petere et cauponem punire."

iterum surrexit Septimus. prima luce ad cauponam ivit et plaustrum petivit. ubi plaustrum invenit, stercus removit et corpus extraxit. Septimus, ubi amicum mortuum vidit, lacrimavit. cauponem statim accusavit. mox cives eum puniverunt.

postquam miles fabulam finivit, silentium fuit. subito Cornelius exclamavit "agite, pueri! nonne vos iussi post cenam cubitum ire? cur ad cubiculum non ivistis?"

sed Marcus "pater, nos quoque fabulam militis audire voluimus. non defessi sumus. non sero est."

hoc tamen dixit Marcus quod cubitum ire timebat. dum enim fabulam militis audiebat, cauponem spectabat. cogitabat: "quam scelestus ille caupo videtur! certe in animo habet media nocte me necare. necesse est vigilare."

etiam Sextus timebat. cogitabat tamen "si hic caupo est scelestus, gaudeo quod miles in caupona pernoctat. Eucleides certe nos adiuvare non potest."

inviti tandem pueri cubitum iverunt, vigilare parati. mox tamen semisomni fuerunt. brevi tempore obdormivit Marcus.

somnus, -i (*m*), sleep
ei, to him
somnium, -i (*n*), dream
postquam, after
animum recuperare, to
    regain one's senses, be fully
    awake
nihil mali, there is nothing
    wrong
obdormio (4), to go to sleep
corpus, corporis (*n*), body

stercus, stercoris (*n*), dung
supra, above, on top
punio (4), to punish
prima luce, at dawn
mortuus, -a, -um, dead
finio (4), to finish
sero, late
cogito (1), to think
videtur, (he) seems
invitus, -a, -um, unwilling

venio, venire (4), **veni, ventum,** to come
surgo, surgere (3), **surrexi, surrectum,** to rise, get up
adiuvo, adiuvare (1), **adiuvi, adiutum,** to help
pono, ponere (3), **posui, positum,** to place
conicio, conicere (3), **conieci, coniectum,** to throw
eo, ire, ivi, itum, to go
peto, petere (3), **petivi, petitum,** to look for, seek
invenio, invenire (4), **inveni, inventum,** to find
removeo, removere (2), **removi, remotum,** to remove
extraho, extrahere (3), **extraxi, extractum,** to drag out
video, videre (2), **vidi, visum,** to see
iubeo, iubere (2), **iussi, iussum,** to order
dico, dicere (3), **dixi, dictum,** to say, tell

Exercise 20a

Responde Latine:
1 ubi est Megara?
2 ubi pernoctavit Aulus? ubi erat amicus Auli?
3 quando Aulus apparuit?   **quando**? when?
4 quid fecit Septimus postquam animum recuperavit?
5 ubi caupo corpus Auli posuit? quid in animo habuit?
6 quid Septimus prima luce fecit?
7 quando lacrimavit Septimus?
8 quid cives fecerunt?
9 cur Sextus gaudebat?
10 quomodo pueri cubitum iverunt?   **quomodo**? how? in
                                              what way?

Exercise 20b

The following sentences contain errors of fact in the light of the last story you read. Explain what is wrong in each sentence:

1 duo pueri, Aulus et Septimus, urbem Romam intraverunt.
2 Aulus et Septimus fratres Marci erant.
3 Septimus media nocte surrexit quod esuriebat.
4 Aulus auxilium petivit quod lectus sordidus erat.
5 cives, postquam Septimum necaverunt, corpus sub stercore celaverunt.
6 caupo Septimum accusavit postquam civem mortuum invenit.
7 Septimus cives punire in animo habuit quod scelesti erant.
8 cives corpus in caupona sub lecto invenerunt.
9 Marcus cubitum ire timuit quod silentium erat.
10 Cornelius cauponem punivit quod Marcus eum accusavit.

Exercise 20c

Using the list of Principal Parts given in Vocabulary 20, write the Latin for:

1 Why have you come?
2 They got up suddenly.
3 The boys went to bed at last.
4 Septimus looked for the cart.
5 What have you seen?
6 We went to the inn.
7 What did you say, Marcus?
8 We ordered Cornelia to go to sleep.
9 What have they found?
10 He placed the body in the cart.

veni, vidi, vici.   *I came, I saw, I conquered.* (Julius Caesar, after the battle of Zela, 47 BC.)

VERBS: Perfect and Imperfect

The imperfect tense describes an action in the past which
    (a) went on for a time, or
    (b) was repeated, or
    (c) was beginning to happen.

The perfect tense describes an action in the past which *happened* or *was completed* on one occasion.

e.g. hoc **dixit** Marcus quod cubitum ire **timebat**.
    Marcus **said** *this because he* **was afraid** *to go to bed.*

    virgam **arripuit** et raedarium **verberabat**.
    He **grabbed** *the stick and* **beat** *the driver* **repeatedly**.

    Cornelii solliciti caelum **spectaverunt** quod iam **advesperascebat**.
    The Cornelii **looked** *anxiously at the sky because it* **was** *already* **getting dark**.

Exercise 20d

Translate with due regard to the tenses of the verb:
1 Marcus sub arbore sedebat, sed subito surrexit.
2 iam advesperascebat ubi viatores aedificia urbis conspexerunt.
3 cauponam non intravimus quod ibi pernoctare timebamus.
4 caupo prope portam laborabat ubi clamorem audivit.
5 ubi Aurelia cubiculum intravit, Cornelia adhuc dormiebat.
6 "tacete, omnes!" exclamavit Davus, nam dominus
    appropinquabat.
7 postquam Aurelia rem explicavit, Eucleides quoque dolebat.
8 tu, Sexte, mox obdormivisti, sed ego diu vigilabam.
9 caupo mussabat quod servos alium lectum petere iussisti.
10 Sextus cauponam statim petivit quod canes latrabant.

21
A Restless Night

Sextus tamen non obdormivit, nam de militis fabula cogitabat. itaque diu vigilabat et de Aulo mortuo cogitabat. tandem "Marce!" inquit. "tune timuisti ubi illam fabulam audivisti?"

sed Marcus nihil respondit. iterum "Marce!" inquit. "tune cauponem spectabas?" iterum silentium! deinde Sextus, iam timidus, "Marce! Marce!" inquit. "cur tu obdormivisti? cur tu non vigilavisti?"

subito sonitum in cubiculo audivit Sextus. "o me miserum! sonitumne audivit Aulus ille miser ubi caupo eum necare parabat? qualis sonitus fuit?"

sonitum Sextus iterum audivit. "o Eucleides!" inquit. "cur ad cubiculum nondum venisti? o pater! o mater! cur me in Italiam misistis? voluistisne ita me ad mortem mittere? in Asiam ego redire volo. ibi enim nullum est periculum, sed periculosum est hic in Italia habitare."

multa se rogavit Sextus, nam, quamquam puer temerarius esse solebat, nunc media nocte solus in cubiculo tremebat.

itaque Sextus, per totam noctem vigilare paratus, diu ibi sedebat. "quomodo iam e manibus cauponis scelesti effugere possum? suntne omnes caupones scelesti? fortasse caupo me, filium civis praeclari, necare in animo habet. quamquam Aulus aurum habuit, ego tamen nihil habeo, neque aurum neque pecuniam."

ita cogitabat Sextus. iterum sonitum audivit. timebat sed tandem surrexit invitus, nam omnes cubiculi partes inspicere volebat. mox tamen risit. ecce! sub lecto erat feles, obesa et semisomna. prope felem Sextus murem mortuum vidit. mùssavit Sextus "non necesse est hoc corpus sub stercore celare!"

sonitus, -us (*m*), sound
ita, in this way
mors, mortis (*f*), death

se rogavit, (he) asked himself, wondered
totus, -a, -um, whole

e manibus, from the hands
aurum, -i (*n*), gold
pecunia, -ae (*f*), money

feles, felis (*f*), cat
mus, muris (*m*), mouse

volo, velle, volui, to wish
tremo, tremere (3), **tremui,** to tremble
inspicio, inspicere (3), **inspexi, inspectum,** to examine

Eavesdropping

It was quite dark. Cornelia was still wide awake. All kinds of
exciting sounds were floating up from the inn downstairs,
inviting her to go down and have a look. She slipped out of bed,
put a shawl round her shoulders and tiptoed into the corridor
where Eucleides was on guard.

"Take me downstairs, Eucleides," she wheedled. "I've never
seen the inside of an inn before." This was quite true, because a
Roman away from home preferred to stay in a friend's villa and
avoided inns if possible.

Eucleides took a lot of persuading, but Cornelia could always
get round him; he soon found himself downstairs, looking into
the main room, with Cornelia peering from behind his arm.

It was pretty dark inside, despite the lamps. The atmosphere
was thick with smoke and reeked of garlic. On the far side
Cornelia could see her father and Marcus and Sextus; and
nearer were other customers seated on stools at rough tables,
and an evil-looking group they were.

"Stay away from them, Cornelia," whispered Eucleides.
"Those rogues would murder their own mothers for a silver
denarius."

But Eucleides needn't have worried because they were all
absorbed in what was going on at the far end of the low room,
where a girl was dancing. Above the hum of conversation her
singing could be heard to the accompaniment of a rhythmic
clacking noise she seemed to be making with her fingers.
"Makes that noise with castanets," whispered Eucleides.
"Dancing girl from Spain, probably Cadiz."

But one person was not paying much attention to the
entertainment—the **tabellarius**, whose reckless driving had
ditched them. He had not come out of the incident unscathed.

One of his horses had gone lame, and he was making the most of the enforced delay, drinking the innkeeper's best Falernian.

As Cornelia and Eucleides entered, the innkeeper was bringing forward a young man to introduce him to the imperial courier. "This is Decimus Junius Juvenalis, sir, a soldier like yourself." The **tabellarius**, unbending slightly as a rather haggard young man came forward wearing the insignia of a junior officer, dismissed the innkeeper with a look and said pleasantly enough, "Greetings, young man! Where are you from?"

"I'm on my way back from service in Britain, sir. What a place! They don't have any climate there, just bad weather! Mist, rain, hail, snow—the lot! Hardly a blink of sunshine!"

"Perhaps he knows our Davus." whispered Cornelia.

"Let me see!" said the **tabellarius**. "Who's governor of Britain these days? A chap called Agricola, I hear."

"That's right!" replied Juvenalis. "A madman, if you ask me. He's not content with conquering the bit of Britain that's near Gaul, where you can get something profitable, like silver or wool or hides or those huge hunting-dogs. Before I left he had gone to the very edge of the world where the Caledonii live. They say that there, in the middle of winter, the sun doesn't shine at all! But I can't vouch for that myself!"

"I've been to Britain too," said the **tabellarius**, much interested. "I'm not an ordinary **tabellarius**, you know. I'm really in charge of a section of the **cursus publicus**. I personally carry dispatches only if they are confidential messages from ..."

And here he whispered something in Juvenalis' ear which Cornelia could not catch.

The innkeeper sidled up again with some more wine.

"We get lots of interesting people stopping here on the Via Appia," he confided. "Not only military gentlemen like yourselves, or that scum of humanity there"—jerking his thumb towards the dancer's audience—"but special envoys to the Emperor himself. When Nero was Emperor, we had one of this new Jewish religious sect who lodged here on a journey all the way from Judaea, to be tried by the Emperor himself no less! He was called Paul or something...."

Suddenly Cornelia felt her ear seized between finger and thumb and looked round into the eyes of a very angry Aurelia. She found herself upstairs and back in bed before she knew what had happened.

22
From the Inn to Rome

iam dies erat. prima luce raedarius auxilio servorum cauponis raedam ex fossa extraxit et ad cauponam admovit. tum servi cistas Corneliorum raedario tradiderunt. interea in caupona, dum Cornelii omnes se parabant, Sextus, iam immemor terroris nocturni, militis fabulam Corneliae narrabat; Eucleides mandata servis dabat. Cornelius ipse Aureliae et liberis clamabat "agite, omnes! nolite cessare! tempus est discedere."

tandem cuncti e caupona venerunt et in raedam ascenderunt.

"vale!" clamaverunt pueri.

"valete!" respondit caupo, qui in area stabat. "nolite in fossam iterum cadere! non in omnibus cauponis bene dormire potestis."

tum raedarius habenas sumpsit et equos verberavit. tandem Romam iterum petebant.

in itinere Sextus omnia de mure mortuo Marco explicavit, Cornelius militis fabulam uxori narravit. iam urbi appropinquabant, cum subito pueri ingens aedificium conspexerunt.

Marcus patrem "quid est illud?" rogavit.

atque Sextus "quis in illo aedificio habitat?"

cui Cornelius "nemo ibi habitat" cum risu respondit. "est sepulcrum Messallae Corvini qui erat orator praeclarus. hic sunt sepulcra multorum et praeclarorum civium quod Romanis non licet intra urbem sepulcra habere."

mox alterum aedificium magnum viderunt.

"estne id quoque sepulcrum, pater?" rogavit Marcus.

"ita vero!" Cornelius respondit. "est sepulcrum Caeciliae Metellae. nonne de Caecilia Metella audivisti?"

sed Marcus patri nihil respondit. iam enim urbem ipsam videre poterat. "ecce Roma!" clamavit.

"ecce Roma! ecce Roma!" clamaverunt Sextus et Cornelia.

tum Cornelius "brevi tempore ad Portam Capenam adveniemus et Titum, patruum vestrum, ibi videbimus. epistolam enim per servum misi et omnia ei explicavi. Titus mox nos prope Portam excipiet."

auxilio, with the help
raedario, to the coachman
se parare, to prepare oneself, get ready
immemor, immemoris, forgetful
nocturnus, -a, -um, during the night
Corneliae, to Cornelia
mandatum, -i (*n*), order, instruction
bene, well
habenae, -arum (*f. pl*), reins

uxori, to his wife
cum, when
ingens, ingentis, huge
illud, that
atque, and
sepulcrum, -i (*n*), tomb
intra (+ *acc.*), inside
adveniemus, we shall come
patruus, -i (*m*), uncle
vester, vestra, vestrum, your
videbimus, we shall see
excipiet, (he) will welcome

trado, tradere (3), **tradidi, traditum,** to hand over
do, dare (1), **dedi, datum,** to give
ascendo, ascendere (3), **ascendi, ascensum,** to climb
respondeo, respondere (2), **respondi, responsum,** to reply
sumo, sumere (3), **sumpsi, sumptum,** to take, take up

The Via Appia and the tomb of Caecilia Metella. (By courtesy of the Italian State Tourist Office (E.N.I.T.).)

NOUNS: Cases and Groups

Dative

Look at the following sentences:

1 omnia **Marco** explicavit.	*He explained everything* **to Marcus**.
2 mandata **servis** dabat.	*He was giving orders* **to the slaves**.
3 fabulam **Corneliae** narrabat.	*He was telling a story* **to Cornelia**.
4 Marcus **patri** nihil respondit.	*Marcus made no reply* **to his father**.
5 Aulus **ei** apparuit.	*Aulus appeared* **to him**.
6 lectum **tibi** paraverunt.	*They have prepared a bed* **for you**.

The Latin words in dark type are all in the *dative case*.

Here is a table showing the Groups and Cases you have met:

		Group 1	Group 2		Group 3	
Sing.	Nom.	puell**a**	serv**us**	puer	vox	pater
	Acc.	puell**am**	serv**um**	puer**um**	voc**em**	patr**em**
	Gen.	puell**ae**	serv**i**	puer**i**	voc**is**	patr**is**
	Dat.	puell**ae**	serv**o**	puer**o**	voc**i**	patr**i**
	Abl.	puell**a**	serv**o**	puer**o**	voc**e**	patr**e**
Plural	Nom.	puell**ae**	serv**i**	puer**i**	voc**es**	patr**es**
	Acc.	puell**as**	serv**os**	puer**os**	voc**es**	patr**es**
	Gen.	puell**arum**	serv**orum**	puer**orum**	voc**um**	patr**um**
	Dat.	puell**is**	serv**is**	puer**is**	voc**ibus**	patr**ibus**
	Abl.	puell**is**	serv**is**	puer**is**	voc**ibus**	patr**ibus**

Notes: 1 In each Group dative and ablative plurals have the same endings.

2 **mihi, tibi, ei, nobis, vobis** and **eis** are the datives of **ego, tu, is, ea, nos, vos** and **ei** (*they*).

3 The dative endings of the adjective are:

	Group 1/2			Group 3		
	Masc.	*Fem.*	*Neut.*	*Masc.*	*Fem.*	*Neut.*
Sing.	magn**o**	magn**ae**	magn**o**	omn**i**	omn**i**	omn**i**
Plur.	magn**is**	magn**is**	magn**is**	omn**ibus**	omn**ibus**	omn**ibus**

Exercise 22a

Translate the following sentence:
Cornelius fabulam uxori narravit.

Now reword the sentence to show that Cornelius told the story to each of the following in turn. (Remember that you must check the Group of each noun before you can produce the correct ending.):
Septimus, Flavia, miles, pueri, raedarius, senatores, caupo, viatores.

Exercise 22b

The sentence **Eucleides mandata servis dabat** can be translated
Eucleides was giving orders to the slaves.
or *Eucleides was giving the slaves orders.*

Translate each of the following sentences in two ways:
1 patruus pecuniam pueris dat.
2 mater fabulam puellae narravit.
3 oratores fabulas civibus narraverunt.
4 ancilla invita cauponi cibum tradit.
5 caupones raro cenam senatoribus dant.   **raro,** seldom
6 omnia patri meo semper dico.
7 nihil legato principis dixit.

NOTE
The dative case is also found with **licet** and **appropinquare**, e.g.
mihi licet exire.   *It is permissible for me to go out.*
                                        I am allowed to go out.
urbi appropinquabant.   *They were coming near to the city.*
                                        They were approaching the city.

Exercise 22c

Translate:
1 matres liberorum multa eis dicunt.
2 Davus Cornelii mandata servis dedit.
3 Cornelii mox urbis portis appropinquabant.
4 Cornelius epistolam ad Titum misit et omnia ei explicavit.
5 pueris non licebat solis per vias errare.
6 Marcus "tace, Sexte!" inquit. "nobis non licet hic clamare."
7 dum Cornelii urbi appropinquabant, Titus omnia eis parabat.

NOUNS: Dative or Ablative?

You will have noticed that the dative and ablative cases often have identical endings, e.g. **servo, puellis, militibus**. How are you to tell which case is used in a particular sentence? Latin will usually provide clues to help you decide correctly:

(*a*) Is the noun preceded by a preposition? If it is, the noun will be in the ablative case because no preposition governs the dative case.

(*b*) If there is no preposition, does the noun refer to a *person*? If it does, it will normally be in the dative because nouns referring to persons are usually governed by a preposition if they are in the ablative. If the noun refers to a *thing*, it is more likely to be ablative than dative.

Consider the sentences, noting the clues provided by each word as you meet it:

1 **canem nostrum puero dedit.**
canem nostrum is obviously accusative. When we reach **puero**, knowing that **puer** refers to a person, we can say that it must be in the dative case because it would be governed by a preposition if it was in the ablative case. A Roman reading as far as **puero** would have known before he reached the verb that someone was transferring "our dog" in some way or other "to the boy".

2 **puero canem nostrum dedimus.**
The fact that **puero** comes first in the sentence does not alter the reasoning. Since it refers to a person and is not governed by a preposition, it must be in the dative case and, again, some transfer is taking place.

3 **canem nostrum baculo verberat.**
When we come to **baculo**, knowing that **baculum** refers to a thing, we can be sure because of the sense that it is in the ablative case. A Roman would have understood as soon as he reached **baculo** that someone was "doing" something to our dog *with* a stick.

4 **baculo canem nostrum verberat.**
Again, the fact that **baculo** appears as the first word makes no difference. We again know that **baculo** must be in the ablative case because it refers to a thing, and when we come to **canem** we know that someone is "doing" something to our dog *with* a stick.

37

Exercise 22d

Look carefully for the type of clue mentioned on page 37 to help you with the words which could be dative or ablative. Then translate the sentences.

1 caupo viatoribus cibum dedit.
2 servus murem baculo necavit.
3 raedarius equos habenis devertebat.
4 amico captivi aurum tradidi.
5 puellae felem baculo vexabant.
6 necesse erat pecuniam praedonibus tradere.
7 pueri pontem in rivo ramis faciebant.
8 epistolas principis tabellariis dedisti.
9 auriga habenas manibus arripuit.
10 senator filiis fabulas narrat.
11 servus nomina virorum domino dixit.
12 boves clamoribus incitamus.
13 vilicus bovem ex rivo manibus extraxit.
14 frater meus captivos auro adiuvit.
15 mercatores togas et tunicas civibus monstrant.

pons, pontis (*m*), bridge

festina lente.	*More hurry, less speed.*
tempus fugit.	*Time flies.*
non omnia possumus omnes.	*We cannot all do everything.*
civis Romanus sum.	*I am a Roman citizen.*

23
At the Porta Capena

interea Titus, patruus Marci et Corneliae, eos prope Portam Capenam exspectabat. cives, mercatores, servi per portam ibant atque huc illuc currebant. Titus tamen in lectica sedebat. ubi Cornelios conspexit, e lectica descendit. e raeda descenderunt Cornelii. interdiu enim raedas intra urbem agere Romanis non licebat.

stupuit Sextus ubi multitudinem civium, servorum turbam vidit. undique erat strepitus plaustrorum, undique clamor mercatorum, viatorum, raedariorum.

Titus Cornelium et Aureliam et liberos maximo cum gaudio salutavit. "quam laetus" inquit "vos omnes excipio! nonne estis itinere defessi?"

"valde defessi" respondit Cornelius. "mihi necesse est celeriter ad Curiam ire, sed primum Aureliam et Corneliam domum ducam."

"ita vero!" inquit Titus. "ecce! lecticarii, quos vobis conduxi, vos domum ferent. ego pueros curabo. multa et mira videbunt pueri, atque ego omnia eis explicabo."

itaque pcr vias urbis lecticarii patrem, matrem, filiam celeriter domum tulerunt. postquam eo advenerunt, Aurelia et Cornelia, itinere defessae, se quieti dederunt. Cornelius tamen se lavit, togam puram induit, iterum in lectica consedit.

"ad Curiam celeriter!" inquit.

mercator, -oris (*m*), merchant	**domum,** home
huc illuc, this way and that	**ducam,** I shall take
lectica, -ae (*f*), litter	**ferent,** (they) will carry
interdiu, during the day	**curabo,** I shall take care of
stupeo (2), to be amazed	**multa et mira,** many
turba, -ae (*f*), crowd	wonderful things
undique, on all sides	**videbunt,** (they) will see
strepitus, -us (*m*), clattering	**eo,** there, to there
maximo cum gaudio, with	**quies, quietis** (*f*), rest
great joy	**purus, -a, -um,** clean
primum, first	**Curia, -ae** (*f*), Senate House

conspicio, conspicere (3), **conspexi, conspectum,** to catch sight of

descendo, descendere (3), **descendi, descensum,** to climb down

ago, agere (3), **egi, actum,** to do, drive

conduco, conducere (3), **conduxi, conductum,** to hire

fero, ferre, tuli, latum, to carry, to bring

induo, induere (3), **indui, indutum,** to put on

consido, considere (3), **consedi, consessum,** to sit down

Slaves carrying a **lectica**

VERBS: Future Tense (1)

Look at these examples taken from story 23:

ego Corneliam domum **ducam**.	**I shall take** *Cornelia home.*
vos domum **ferent**.	**They will carry** *you home.*
multa et mira **videbunt** pueri.	*The boys* **will see** *many wonderful things.*
ego omnia eis **explicabo**.	**I shall explain** *everything to them.*

The words in dark type are examples of the *future tense*. The endings of the future tense are shown in the table below:

Groups 1 and 2		Groups 3 and 4	
-bo		**-am**	
-bis		**-es**	
-bit		**-et**	
-bimus		**-emus**	
-bitis		**-etis**	
-bunt		**-ent**	
para**bo**	habe**bo**	mitt**am**	audi**am**
para**bis**	habe**bis**	mitt**es**	audi**es**
para**bit**	habe**bit**	mitt**et**	audi**et**
para**bimus**	habe**bimus**	mitt**emus**	audi**emus**
para**bitis**	habe**bitis**	mitt**etis**	audi**etis**
para**bunt**	habe**bunt**	mitt**ent**	audi**ent**

Note that in the future tense the endings of verbs in Groups 3 and 4 are quite different from the endings of verbs in Groups 1 and 2.

Exercise 23a

Translate:

1 Titus nos prope Portam Capenam exspectabit; omnes maximo cum gaudio salutabit.
2 hodie sepulcra magna Romanorum praeclarorum vidimus; cras amphitheatrum et alia aedificia Romana videbimus.
3 fortasse patruus noster nos ad Circum Maximum ducet.
4 Cornelii omnes se parant; brevi tempore ad urbem iter facient.
5 raedarius habenas sumit; tandem a caupona discedemus.
6 Eucleidem de Caecilia Metella rogabimus.
7 quam diu in urbe manebis, pater?
8 bene dormietis, pueri. longum enim iter hodie fecistis.
9 Cornelia, itinere longo defessa, se quieti dabit.
10 pueri multa rogabunt de aedificiis quae in urbis viis videbunt.

Exercise 23b

Add to each sentence, as appropriate, **heri, hodie** *or* **cras** *and translate:*

1 milites ad urbem _____ veniunt.
2 pueros parentes ad Circum _____ miserunt.
3 multi homines in via _____ stabunt.
4 multi homines ad portam _____ venient.
5 multae matres laetae _____ erant.
6 senatores milites _____ inspiciunt.
7 aedificia multa _____ vidimus.
8 cur non cauponem _____ petemus?
9 nos omnes _____ risimus.
10 nos omnes _____ dormiemus.

Exercise 23c

Translate:

1 "quam ingens est Roma!" inquit Marcus. "certe non visitabimus omnia urbis aedificia."
2 Titus multas fabulas de aedificiis Romae pueris narrabit.
3 mox urbi appropinquabunt et patruum conspicient.
4 "nonne timebas, Sexte, in caupona dormire?" "minime vero!" respondit Sextus. "ego numquam timeo."
5 "heri in itinere" inquit Marcus "multa vehicula videbam sed mox ingentia aedificia urbis videbo."
6 diu per vias urbis ambulavimus; quando ad Circum Maximum veniemus?
7 cras, ubi surgetis, pueri, strepitum plaustrorum audietis.
8 pueri, ubi domum advenient, cenam habebunt et mox dormient.
9 Titus Cornelium fratrem exspectabit; tum multa de itinere audiet.
10 Cornelia Aureliam rogat "quid nos cras agemus, mater?"

Exercise 23d (Revision)

interea Eucleides et pueri cum Tito extra Portam Capenam stabant.

TITUS: salvete, pueri! quid in itinere vidistis? vidistisne rusticos in agris? agrosne colebant?

SEXTUS: rusticos vidimus. agros non colebant, sed sub arboribus quiescebant. at cauponam vidimus; nostra
raeda in fossa haerebat et nobis necesse erat in
caupona pernoctare.
MARCUS: ita vero! gaudebam quod pater meus in illa caupona
pernoctare constituit. caupo erat vir Graecus, amicus
Eucleidis.
SEXTUS: ego quoque gaudebam, nam miles bonam fabulam
nobis narravit. in illa fabula caupo quidam hospitem
necavit. tales fabulas amo.
MARCUS: sed quid nunc faciemus, patrue? ego volo Curiam et
forum videre.
SEXTUS: quando Circum Maximum visitabimus? ecce! nonne
Circum Maximum supra muros urbis exstantem
videre possum?
MARCUS: ita vero! est Circus Maximus. non procul abest.
TITUS: non possumus omnia hodie videre. cras satis temporis
habebimus.
SEXTUS: sed quid est illud aedificium? nonne pontem ingentem
supra portam video?
MARCUS: non pontem hic vides, o stulte! est aquaeductus, Aqua
Marcia. per illum aquaeductum Romani aquam in
urbem ferunt. cave imbrem, Sexte!
SEXTUS: sed non pluit.
TITUS: semper hic pluit, Sexte. rimosa enim est Aqua Marcia.

at, but

talis, talis, tale, such

quando? when?

supra (+ *acc.*), above

murus, -i (*m*), wall

exstantem, standing out,
  towering

satis temporis, enough time

pons, pontis (*m*), bridge

stultus, -a, -um, stupid

aqua, -ae (*f*), water

cave imbrem! Watch out
  for the rain!

pluit, it is raining

rimosus, a, -um, full of
  cracks

colo, colere (3), **colui, cultum,** to cultivate
constituo, constituere (3), **constitui, constitutum,** to decide

43

Aqueducts

One feature of the city which the Cornelii would notice as they approached Rome was the evidence of the Romans' passion for water. Abundant water for baths and fountains and lakes was an utter necessity to the Roman, so that it had to be brought in by the aqueducts whose arches strode into Rome from all directions. By AD 80 nine aqueducts were in use, carrying water across the plain to Rome from sources up to ninety kilometres distant.

The illustration shows the arches supporting the water-channel and a cross-section of the channel itself. To maintain the downhill flow, experts recommended a fall of fifteen centimetres in every thirty metres. Tunnels, with inspection shafts built into them, were driven through hills which it was impossible to by-pass. Sometimes, by using the principle that water rises to its own level, a U-shaped arrangement of the

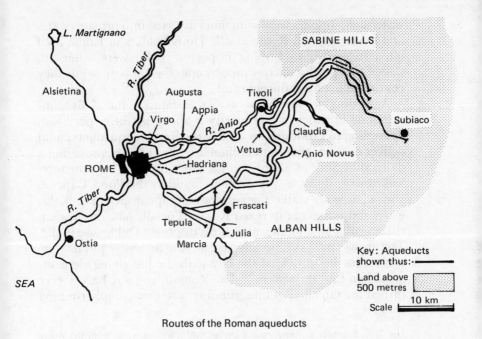

Routes of the Roman aqueducts

tunnel allowed an uphill flow. Responsibility for maintaining and cleaning the whole vast system rested with the **curator aquarum** and his staff.

The first aqueduct, the **Aqua Appia**, went underground but since a gravity system was employed, later ones had to be higher to serve the hillier districts of the town. The Romans then hit on the idea of using arches to support the water-channel. The arches turned out to be beautiful structures in themselves but the Romans had adopted them for quite different reasons. They stood up better to earthquakes, always a hazard in Italy; the wind could blow through them, where a solid wall would invite disaster; they could be easily repaired as workmen could take the building materials from one side to the other.

Admiring comments about the aqueducts abound from native and foreigner alike. "Just as impressive," says one writer, "as the pyramids, but how much more useful!" Not only so, but we also have an astonishing book, *De Aquis Urbis Romae*, by Frontinus, Superintendent of Aqueducts, written about AD 97, describing the system in detail and the difficulties of organising and maintaining it. He reports that, through bribery of watermen, supplies were sometimes diverted into private estates and never reached Rome at all. Householders in Rome itself often succeeded in bribing inspectors (who were, after all, slaves) to replace a narrow pipe by one of wider bore, while they continued to pay at the old rate!

According to the latest available figures, the daily consumption of water in a large city is about 455 litres per head. According to Frontinus, in his day the Roman aqueducts could deliver over one thousand million litres in 24 hours, providing a daily allowance of about 900 litres per head! The aqueducts leaked dreadfully, as the Cornelii found at the Porta Capena, and what with water thieves and corrupt inspectors all this water did not actually reach Rome. For all that, the Roman citizen still had a lot of water at his disposal. Did he use it all? The answer is "Yes", because as one Roman writer put it "The waters, having provided the city with the life-giving element, passed on into the sewers." The Roman, you see, hardly ever turned the tap off. For him, running water was simply running water!

The Trevi fountain in Rome, still supplied with running water from the **Aqua Virgo**. (The Mansell Collection.)

VERBS: Future Tense (2)

The following are the future tenses of the irregular verbs you have met:

esse	posse	ire	velle	nolle
ero	pot**ero**	i**bo**	vol**am**	nol**am**
eris	pot**eris**	i**bis**	vol**es**	nol**es**
erit	pot**erit**	i**bit**	vol**et**	nol**et**
erimus	pot**erimus**	i**bimus**	vol**emus**	nol**emus**
eritis	pot**eritis**	i**bitis**	vol**etis**	nol**etis**
erunt	pot**erunt**	i**bunt**	vol**ent**	nol**ent**

Exercise 23e

Translate:

1 ibisne ad Curiam, pater? ita vero! ad Curiam celeriter ibo.
2 quando domum redibis, pater? nescio.
3 fortasse Cornelius domum redire brevi tempore poterit.
4 Eucleides ad amphitheatrum ire nolet.
5 necesse erit diu in urbe manere.
6 si pluet, ad silvam ambulare nolam.
7 ad villam mox redibimus.
8 pueri Circum Maximum cras videre volent.
9 ubi liberi mane erunt? tu liberos non videbis, nam e domo mox exibunt.
10 si equi raedam e fossa extrahent, Cornelii ad urbem iter facere poterunt.

e domo, out of the house

24
Always Tomorrow

simulac Titus et pueri et Eucleides urbem per Portam Capenam intraverunt, clamavit Sextus "quid nos primum faciemus? quo ibimus? visitabimusne ... ?"

"quo tu nos duces, patrue?" interpellavit Marcus. "videbimusne Curiam et forum?"

Titus "tacete! tacete!" inquit. "forum cras visitabimus. cras, Eucleides, tibi licebit pueros eo ducere. tum erit satis temporis. hodie tamen, pueri, vos domum per urbem ducam et omnia in itinere vobis demonstrabo."

iam advenerant ad Circum Maximum, qui non procul aberat. stupuit Sextus ubi molem Circi Maximi vidit. stupuit quoque Marcus, quamquam Circum antea viderat. stupuit Titus, attonitus non mole, sed silentio Circi.

"eheu! eheu!" inquit Titus. "hodie Circus est clausus. tribus diebus tamen princeps ipse ludos magnificos faciet."

"nonne tu nos eo duces?" rogavit Marcus.

"eheu! ego non potero vos ducere" inquit Titus. "fortasse Eucleides vos ducet."

"minime!" respondit Sextus. "libros, non ludos amat Eucleides."

"agite, pueri!" interpellavit Titus. "nunc transibimus Montem Palatinum et descendemus ad arcum Titi. ibi fortasse patri tuo occurremus, Marce. mox senatores ex Curia exibunt."

itaque Circum reliquerunt et Palatinum transierunt. Titus in itinere monstravit pueris mira aedificia quae principes in Palatino aedificaverant. tandem ad arcum Titi advenerunt, iam labore et aestu defessi.

"hic est novus arcus" inquit Titus "quem senatus ..."

"omnia videre poteritis cras" interpellavit Cornelius, qui eo ipso tempore ad arcum ex Curia advenerat. "Eucleides omnia vobis explicabit. iam sero est. agite! iam domum ibimus."

simulac, as soon as
advenerant, they had arrived

moles, molis (*f*), mass. huge bulk

viderat, he had seen

attonitus, -a, -um, astonished

clausus, -a, -um, closed

ludi, -orum (*m.pl*), games

liber, libri (*m*), book

arcus, -us (*m*), arch

aedifico (1), to build

aestu, by the heat

quem (*acc.*), which

occurro, occurrere (3), **occurri, occursum** (+ *dat.*), to meet, encounter

relinquo, relinquere (3), **reliqui, relictum,** to leave

transeo, transire, transii, transitum, to go across

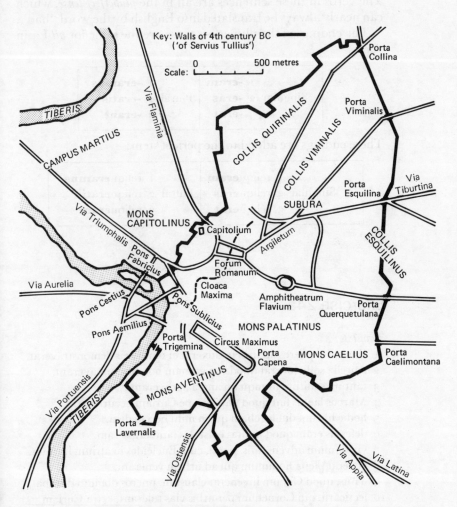

Map of Rome at the end of the first century B.C.

VERBS: Pluperfect Tense

Look at these sentences:

iam **advenerant** ad Circum.	*They* **had** *already* **reached** *the Circus*.
Circum antea **viderat**.	*He* **had seen** *the Circus before*.
mira aedificia **aedificaverant**.	*They* **had built** *marvellous buildings*.

The verbs in these sentences are all in the *pluperfect tense*, which can nearly always be translated into English by the word "had".

The endings of the pluperfect tense are the same for *all* Latin verbs:

	1	**-eram**		1	**-eramus**
Singular	2	**-eras**	Plural	2	**-eratis**
	3	**-erat**		3	**-erant**

These endings are added to the perfect stem:

	1	reliqu**eram**		1	reliqu**eramus**
Singular	2	reliqu**eras**	Plural	2	reliqu**eratis**
	3	reliqu**erat**		3	reliqu**erant**

Exercise 24a

Translate:

1. Eucleides pueros ad urbem duxerat et omnia eis demonstraverat.
2. Aurelia sollicita erat quod servi cenam nondum paraverant.
3. tantum sonitum numquam antea audiveramus.
4. Marcus laetus fuit quod patri prope Curiam occurrerat.
5. hodie librum diu legebam quem mihi heri dedisti.
6. defessus eram quod multas epistolas iam scripseram.
7. vix domum adveneratis, pueri, cum Eucleides in atrium intravit.
8. via erat plena hominum qui ad urbem venerant.
9. Titus, quod Circum invenerat clausum, pueros domum ducebat.
10. lecticarii, qui Cornelium per urbis vias tulerant, extra Curiam eum exspectabant.

VERBS: Present or Future?

Look at these sentences:

Cornelius multos servos hab**et**.	*Cornelius* **has** *many slaves.*
scelestos servos ad villam mitt**et**.	*He* **will send** *the wicked slaves to the farm.*
hodie in caupona man**emus**.	*Today we* **remain** *in the inn.*
cras Romam adveni**emus**.	*Tomorrow we* **shall reach** *Rome.*

The endings **-es**, **-et**, **-emus**, **-etis**, **-ent** can denote the present tense of verbs belonging to Group 2 or the future tense of verbs belonging to Groups 3 or 4.

Exercise 24b

Complete the following table:

Verb	Group Number	Tense	Meaning
habent	2	present	they have
mittent	3	future	they will send
vident			
iubent			
ascendent			
admovent			
dicent			
timent			
ducent			
rident			
facient			

Exercise 24c

Look carefully at the verbs in the following sentences. Decide the Group number first (this will help you to get the tense right) and then translate:

1 pueri Eucleidem non vident, sed vocem eius audient.
2 videsne senatores in viis? quando Cornelius veniet?
3 servi celeriter current, nam Cornelium timent.
4 Sextus mane surget; in animo habet exire.
5 ego et Cornelia tacemus; patrem timemus.

25
First Morning in Rome

iam dies erat. magnus erat clamor in urbe. iam canes in viis latrabant, iam homines clamabant et per vias currebant. servi ad forum magno tumultu onera ferebant. undique clamor et strepitus! sed nihil clamoris, nihil strepitus ad Marcum pervenit. neque clamores hominum neque latratus canum eum excitaverant. in lecto stertebat nam defessus erat.

Sextus quoque in lecto manebat sed dormire non poterat. numquam antea urbem tantam visitaverat. clamoribus et strepitu excitatus, iam cogitabat de omnibus rebus quas Titus heri narraverat. "quid hodie videbimus? fortasse cum Tito ibimus qui omnia nobis demonstrabit. Corneliusne nos in forum ducet? ego certe forum et Curiam et senatores videre volo."

interea Eucleides, qui prima luce exierat, iam domum redierat. statim cubiculum puerorum petivit et "eho, pueri!" inquit. "cur nondum surrexistis? abhinc duas horas ego surrexi. quod novum librum emere volebam, in Argiletum mane descendi ad tabernam quandam ubi in postibus nomina multorum poetarum videre potes. Catullus, Flaccus..."

at pueri celeriter interpellaverunt quod Eucleides, ut bene sciebant, semper aliquid docere volebat. "quid in via vidisti?"

Eucleides "nihil" inquit "nisi miserum hominem lapidibus oppressum. boves lapides quadratos in plaustro trahebant ad novum aedificium quod Caesar prope Domum Auream aedificat. illud aedificium est ingens amphitheatrum et mox ..."

at pueri in cubiculo non iam manebant, nam Eucleides, qui erat semper verbosus, multa de aedificiis urbis narrare solebat; neque tamen pueri eum audire volebant.

tumultus, -us, (*m*) noise, uproar	**abhinc duas horas,** two hours ago
tantus, -a, -um, so great	
excitatus, -a, -um, aroused	**taberna, -ae** (*f*), shop
de omnibus rebus, about all the things, about everything	**ad tabernam quandam,** to a shop

postis, postis (*m*), door-post
ut bene sciebant, as they
  well knew
aliquid, something
lapidibus oppressum,
  crushed by stones

lapides quadrati, squared
  stones
quod, which
Domus Aurea, (Nero's)
  Golden House
at, but
neque tamen, but ... not

pervenio, pervenire (4), **perveni, perventum,** to arrive (at),
  reach
sterto, stertere (3), **stertui,** to snore
emo, emere (3), **emi, emptum,** to buy
doceo, docere (2), **docui, doctum,** to teach

NOUNS: Groups 4 and 5

Most Latin nouns belong to Groups 1, 2 or 3. There are two
other Groups to which a few nouns belong:

		Group 4	Group 5
	Nom.	man**us**	di**es**
	Acc.	man**um**	di**em**
Singular	Gen.	man**us**	di**ei**
	Dat.	man**ui**	di**ei**
	Abl.	man**u**	di**e**
	Nom.	man**us**	di**es**
	Acc.	man**us**	di**es**
Plural	Gen.	man**uum**	di**erum**
	Dat.	man**ibus**	di**ebus**
	Abl.	man**ibus**	di**ebus**

Nouns of Groups 4 and 5 will appear in vocabularies as follows:

manus, -us (*f*), hand
sonitus, -us (*m*), sound
arcus, -us (*m*), arch
tumultus, -us (*m*), uproar

dies, -ei (*m*), day
res, rei (*f*), thing
meridies, -ei (*m*), midday

Exercise 25a

Translate:

1 media nocte tumultum magnum audivi. quae erat causa huius
tumultus? magno cum strepitu boves plaustra per vias trahebant.
primum strepitus procul aberat; deinde in via nostra erat
tumultus.

    huius, genitive of **hic**

2 multas res manibus nostris facimus. Eucleides manu stilum
tenebat, nam pueros scribere docebat. pueri arbores manibus et
pedibus antea ascenderant. manus igitur eorum sordidae erant.
Eucleides eos iussit manus statim lavare.

    stilus, -i (*m*), pen   **eorum,** their

3 abhinc multos dies illa domus incensa est. itaque dominus, quod
muri domus infirmi erant, domum novam ibi aedificare constituit.
ille dominus est senator qui multas domus in urbe habet. omnes
eius domus sunt magnae, sed domus nova erit omnium maxima. in
hac domo senator ipse habitabit.

    domus, -us (*f*), house   **incensa est,** was burned

4 multos dies in villa manebamus. venit tamen dies reditus. necesse
erat iter septem dierum facere quod ad urbem celerrime redire
volebamus. eo die discessimus. sex dies per viam Appiam iter
faciebamus. septimo die Romam pervenimus.

    reditus, -us (*m*), return

5 Titus rem miram nobis narravit. servus, qui nocte per vias urbis
ambulabat, subito fugit perterritus. quae erat causa huius rei? in
via occurrerat cani qui, ut ipse dixit, tria capita habebat. de
talibus rebus in libris saepe legimus sed numquam talem rem ipsi
vidimus. de hac re omnes cives multas fabulas narrant.

    caput, capitis (*n*), head

ante meridiem   *before mid-day*
post meridiem   *after mid-day*

Rome

Impressions of Rome

What nation is so far distant, Caesar, or so barbarous that it does not have a representative at the games here in your city? Here come farmers from the Balkans, natives of South Russia nurtured on horse's blood, people from the banks of the Nile as well as those from the Atlantic's farthest shores. Here too are Arabs, men from Southern Turkey, German tribesmen and Ethiopians—all so different in dress and in appearance. Their speech too sounds all different; yet it is all one when you are hailed, Caesar, as the true father of our country.

Martial, de Spectaculis III

Caecilius, in your own eyes you are a polished gentleman, but take my word for it, you are not. What are you then? A clown! You are like the hawker from across the Tiber who trades pale brimstone matches for broken glass or the man who sells to the idle bystanders soggy pease-pudding; like the keeper and trainer of snakes or the cheap slaves of the salt-sellers; like the hoarse-voiced seller of smoking sausages with his hot trays or a third-grade street poet.

Martial, Epigrams I.41

If duty calls, the crowd gives way and the rich man is borne along rapidly over their heads by stout Liburnian bearers and on the way will read, write or sleep, for with the windows shut the litter induces sleep. Even so, he will get there before us; though we hurry, the sea of humanity in front hinders us and the great throng following jostles our backs. One man strikes us with his elbow, another with a hard pole; one knocks a beam against our heads, another a barrel. Our legs are plastered with mud, we are trampled on all sides by great feet, a soldier's hob-nailed boot crushes my toe. Newly patched togas are torn; a tall fir tree sways as the wagon rumbles on and the other carts carry pine trees, a nodding menace over the heads of the crowd; for if the cart carrying Ligurian stone tilts forward and pours its overturned pile on the crowds, what remains of their bodies?

Juvenal, Satires III.239

Finding the Way

Roman houses were neither named nor numbered. Hence the
very complicated instructions given to those wishing to reach a
certain "address":

> Every time you meet me, Lupercus, you ask "May I send a slave
> to fetch your book of poems? I'll return it as soon as I've read it."
> Lupercus, it is not worth troubling your slave. It is a long journey
> to the Pear Tree and I live up three flights of steep stairs. You can
> find what you want closer to home. No doubt you often go down
> to the Argiletum. There is a shop opposite Caesar's Forum with
> both door-posts covered with advertisements so that you can in a
> moment read the names of all the poets. Look for me there.
>
> Martial, *Epigrams I.117*

SYRUS: I don't know the man's name but I know where he lives.

DEMEA: Then tell me where.

SYRUS: Down here. You know the colonnade by the butcher's?

DEMEA: Of course I do.

SYRUS: Go straight up the street that way; a bit along there's a slope facing you; down there and after that, on this side here, there's a shrine with an alley beside it.

DEMEA: Where?

SYRUS: Near where the big wild fig-tree grows.

DEMEA: I've got it.

SYRUS: Down there.

DEMEA: But that's a dead end!

SYRUS: Ugh! What an idiot I am! I've made a mistake. Come right back to the colonnade again. Here's a much quicker and more direct route. Do you know the house of rich Cratinus?

DEMEA: Yes.

SYRUS: Go past it, down a street to the left; turn right at Diana's temple. Before you reach the gate, near the pool, there's a bakery with a carpenter's opposite. He's there.

Terence, *Adelphi 571*

57

Columns and Porticos

The column was one of the main features of Roman architecture. Sometimes a single column was used to support a statue; more often, columns were used to support the roofs or to form the entrance-porches of temples and other buildings.

From the idea of the porch, there developed the portico or long covered walk which afforded the citizens protection from sun and dust, while allowing them to enjoy the fresh air. In the shelter of the portico various activities took place. The Portico of Minucius was used as a corn-exchange; in another a vegetable market was held. In the porticos philosophers lectured, poets recited, schoolmasters held their classes, lawyers met their clients, entertainers performed, snacks were sold and business deals were concluded. In fact, porticos became so common that it was eventually possible to walk from one end of the city to the other without coming out into the open at all!

According to one writer, porticos covered more than a quarter of the total area of the Campus Martius, the number of columns supporting them being about 2000. Halls built in the shelter of these housed wall-maps of Rome and the Roman world, exhibitions of wonders from the Far East, natural marvels such as a snake 21 metres long and, in the Portico of Philippus, a display of wigs and the latest in ladies' hairstyles.

Exercise 25b (Revision)

SEXTUS: quam defessus sum, Marce! nam hodie mane dormire non poteram. tantus clamor in viis erat.

MARCUS: qualem clamorem audivisti? ego certe nihil clamoris audivi.

SEXTUS: quid? nonne audivisti illos canes in viis latrantes? multas horas latrabant. numquam audivi tantum strepitum. audivi etiam clamorem multorum hominum qui per vias currebant.

MARCUS: quid clamabant?

SEXTUS: id audire non poteram, nam omnes simul clamabant. certe tamen irati erant. erat quoque strepitus plaustrorum. nos in urbe heri plaustra non vidimus. unde venerunt plaustra?

MARCUS: interdiu non licet plaustra intra urbem agere. nocte igitur necesse est laborare. servi in urbem ferebant cibum, vinum, lapides, . . .

SEXTUS: cur lapides intra urbem tulerunt?

MARCUS: Caesar constituit ingens amphitheatrum in urbe aedificare.

SEXTUS: nos illud aedificium vidimus?

MARCUS: heri illud conspexisti, ubi ad forum cum patre meo ibamus. heri non satis temporis erat id inspicere quod pater domum festinabat. sed mox amphitheatrum iterum visitabimus atque id inspiciemus. fortasse Eucleides nos ducet.

SEXTUS: dum hoc mihi dicis, multi homines in domum venerunt. qui sunt?

MARCUS: nonne heri in urbe vidisti multos cives post senatorem sequentes? hic erat patronus, illi erant clientes. pater meus est patronus multorum civium. tu audivisti clientes domum intrantes.

SEXTUS: eheu! Eucleides quoque intravit!

latrantes, barking   **sequentes,** following
vinum, -i (*n*), wine

patroni were wealthy men who gave food or money to their dependants (**clientes**). The **clientes** came to the patron's home early in the morning to receive this dole and then escorted him to the Forum.

Eucleides the Statistician

Marcus had always visualised himself showing Sextus round the city of Rome, but he should have realised that Cornelius would never allow Sextus and himself to wander round Rome unsupervised. If neither Cornelius nor Titus was free to act as guide, Eucleides was bound to be their companion. He certainly knew a lot; the trouble was, there was no stopping him . . . .

"Rome," Eucleides was now saying in that affected Greek voice of his, "is built on seven hills, the most famous being the Capitol and the Palatine. By now, of course, it has far outstripped these petty limits. Augustus divided it into fourteen regions, which are in turn subdivided into 265 **vici** or wards. At the last census the population numbered 1 284 602, living in 1 797 **domus** and 46 602 **insulae**. . . ."

"I can't see any islands!" complained Sextus, in all seriousness.

"**Insulae**," explained Eucleides, "are those ramshackle tenements where all the riff-raff live."

"And **Insula Feliculae** is the biggest in the world," said Marcus.

"There are," said Eucleides, "96 kilometres of streets. . . ."

"Not very wide, are they?" commented Sextus.

"Maximum width according to *The Twelve Tables* was only five metres," went on Eucleides.

"And some of them are not even paved!" cried Sextus, peering along the dark tunnel they were now traversing between the **insulae**.

"Watch out!" yelled Marcus, pulling Sextus and Eucleides close to the wall to dodge a deluge of slops from a third-floor window.

"We'll have the law on you for that!" shouted Marcus up at the unseen law-breaker. But Eucleides, not anxious to linger bandying threats, hustled the boys off through the labyrinth of shadowy alleys.

Suddenly they emerged into the blinding sun of a piazza.

"This," said Eucleides impressively, pointing to a massive column, "is the centre of the universe, the *Golden Milestone*. Erected by Augustus, it bears upon it in letters of gilt bronze the distances to all the cities of the Empire."

But it was not the *Golden Milestone* the boys were looking at, nor was it the splendour of the Capitol behind them. They were gazing down at the **Forum Romanum** which glittered with marble and bronze and gold. Senators and businessmen with their slaves were hurrying in and out of the **basilicae** that flanked the Forum. The noise was deafening. Cries of sausage-sellers and pastry-vendors mingled with the uproar of every language under heaven. White toga and tunic jostled with all kinds of colours of outlandish garb.

Eucleides, sensing their preoccupation, was just pursing his lips to launch out on a lecture on the Forum; but Marcus and Sextus were off, scampering along the **Via Sacra**.

"Come and tell us what's going on here!" they shouted, running to the far end of the Forum where their attention had been caught by the feverish activity of an army of masons engaged, amidst mountains of rubble and building stone, in some mammoth task of demolition or construction—it was hard to tell which.

"The Emperor Nero ..." began Eucleides breathlessly as he caught up with them.

"I know," said Marcus. "He's the one that set Rome on fire for fun."

"The Emperor Nero," Eucleides repeated, "on the space cleared of unsightly hovels by a quite accidental fire, built the wonderful **Domus Aurea**...."

"And they're still working at it by the look of it!" said Sextus, grinning.

"No, you idiot!" said Marcus. "Vespasian and Titus pulled down Nero's folly and are putting up things for the citizens of Rome to enjoy, baths, for instance, and a huge arch showing Titus' capture of Jerusalem."

"And that terrific statue over there?" pointed Sextus.

"That was a statue of Nero himself," Marcus went on, "but Vespasian put rays round its head and made it into a sun-god statue."

"It is forty metres high," began Eucleides, but his hearers were gone again, towards an immense building under construction.

"What's this?" they asked, as an exhausted Eucleides caught up with them.

"This is the **Amphitheatrum Flavium**" he gasped. "The Emperor Titus is to dedicate it in June."

26
A Grim Lesson

Eucleides et pueri iam domum redierant. post cenam Cornelius et Marcus et Sextus in atrio sedebant.

"quid hodie vidistis, pueri?" inquit Cornelius.

"nihil nisi aedificia antiqua" respondit Marcus. "nos in urbem exire volumus soli. cur non licet?"

cui Cornelius "est periculosum sine custode exire in vias huius urbis. sunt multi homines scelesti qui bona civium arripiunt. nonnumquam hi homines cives ipsos necant. vobis igitur non licet sine custode exire. iam sero est. nunc necesse est vobis cubitum ire. nolite cessare sed ite statim!"

pueri, labore diei defessi, simulac cubitum iverunt, obdormiverunt.

postridie mane Marcus in lecto suo iacebat et de Circo Maximo ita cogitabat: "quando Circum Maximum visitabimus? cur pater meus nos exire vetat? heri nullos homines scelestos in urbe vidi. interdiu certe praedones nobis non nocebunt. meum patrem, quod est senator Romanus, praedones timent. nihil periculi est."

brevi tempore, ut Marco videbatur, pueri ad Circum ibant. mox molem ingentem Circi Maximi Marcus conspexit.

"ecce!" clamavit Marcus. "est Circus. mox intrabimus et aurigas ipsos spectabimus."

subito tamen in viam se praecipitaverunt tres homines.

"cave illos homines!" clamavit Sextus. "illi certe nos in domus vicinas trahent et ibi nos necabunt."

sed frustra, nam Marcus, metu commotus, postquam Sextum audivit clamantem, ad terram cecidit et iacebat in luto immobilis.

"eho!" clamavit unus ex praedonibus. "quo abis, parvule? quid est nomen tuum? nonne tu filius es senatoris? nonne nomen tuum est Marcus Cornelius?"

cui Marcus "quid vultis, scelesti? nihil pecuniae habeo. nolite mihi nocere! si me verberabitis, pater meus certe vos puniet."

sed interpellavit praedo "tace, puer! tu es captivus noster neque ad patrem redibis. nemo nunc poterit te servare. ipse enim te necabo."

tum praedo gladium strinxit. Marcus stabat perterritus et "fer auxilium!" clamavit. "fer auxilium!" sed nemo clamorem audivit. nemo auxilium tulit. Marcus oculos clausit et mortem exspectabat.

nihil accidit. oculos aperuit. in lecto erat suo. somnium modo fuerat. hodie tamen domi manere constituit Marcus.

custos, custodis (*m*), guard
huius, genitive of **hic**
bona, bonorum (*n.pl*),
   goods, possessions
nonnumquam, sometimes
postridie, on the following
   day
iaceo (2), to lie
praedo, praedonis (*m*),
   robber
noceo (2) (+ *dat.*), to harm
ut Marco videbatur, as it
   seemed to Marcus, as
   Marcus thought

metu commotus, in a panic
terra, -ae (*f*), earth, ground
lutum, -i (*n*), mud
parvulus, -a, -um, little
servo (1), to save
gladium strinxit, (he) drew
   his sword
oculus, -i (*m*), eye
accidit, (it) happened
domi, at home

veto, vetare (1), **vetui, vetitum,** to forbid
cado, cadere (3), **cecidi, casum,** to fall
claudo, claudere (3), **clausi, clausum,** to shut
aperio, aperire (4), **aperui, apertum,** to open
sum, esse, fui, to be

hic and ille

Look at the following sentences:

ille tabellarius equos vehementer incitavit.	*That courier fiercely whipped the horses on.*
quis in **illo** aedificio habitat?	*Who lives in **that** building **over there**?*
hi canes latrant modo.	*These dogs are only barking.*
est periculosum in vias **huius** urbis exire.	*It is dangerous to go out into the streets of **this** city.*
Sextus, **his** clamoribus et **hoc** strepitu excitatus, dormire non poterat.	*Roused by **these** shouts and **this** noise, Sextus could not sleep.*

You will see from the above examples that both **hic** and **ille** are used to point out someone or something. **hic** points to someone or something near at hand or near in time, while **ille** points to someone or something further away or "over there" or distant in time.

Here is a table showing all the cases of **hic** and **ille** in masculine, feminine and neuter genders:

		Masc.	Fem.	Neut.	Masc.	Fem.	Neut.
	Nom.	hic	haec	hoc	ille	illa	illud
	Acc.	hunc	hanc	hoc	illum	illam	illud
S	Gen.	huius	huius	huius	illius	illius	illius
	Dat.	huic	huic	huic	illi	illi	illi
	Abl.	hoc	hac	hoc	illo	illa	illo
	Nom.	hi	hae	haec	illi	illae	illa
	Acc.	hos	has	haec	illos	illas	illa
P	Gen.	horum	harum	horum	illorum	illarum	illorum
	Dat.	his	his	his	illis	illis	illis
	Abl.	his	his	his	illis	illis	illis

Exercise 26a

Translate:

1 vidistine libros in illa taberna?
2 ubi nomen illius poetae vidisti? in postibus tabernae vidi.
3 cur sub hac arbore sedes, Cornelia?
4 in hoc lecto dormire nolo.
5 hi viatores in illa caupona non pernoctaverunt.
6 quando ad hanc urbem advenisti, mi amice?
7 ego haec omnia patri meo dicam.
8 cibum huic puellae dabimus quod esurit.
9 sonitumne audivit Aulus ille miser ubi caupo eum necare parabat?
10 hi cives per vias currunt, illi prope tabernas stant.
11 Eucleides cum pueris illi aedificio heri appropinquabat.
12 in hoc libro omnes servi sunt scelesti, in illo sunt boni.

Engraving on a church bell (campana) at Dunning, near Perth in Scotland:

soli Deo gloria, Joannes Oaderogge me fecit Rotterdam 1681	*To God alone (be) the glory; Joannes Oaderogge made me in Rotterdam in 1681.*
haec ad evangelium,	*This (bell) calls sinners to the Gospel.*
hoc ad Christum,	*This (Gospel) calls sinners to Christ.*
Hic ad coelum vocat peccatores.	*He calls sinners to Heaven.*

27

A Visit to the Races

Chariot-racing (**ludi circenses**) was perhaps the most popular spectacle in ancient Rome. It was held in the **Circus Maximus**, a huge open-air stadium in the valley between the Palatine and the Aventine hills. It could hold about 200000 spectators, seated in tiers round the long course (**arena**).

It has been estimated that at one time some 90 holidays (**feriae**) were given over to games at public expense. On these days the citizens were "on holiday" (**feriati**).

A barrier (**spina**) ran down the centre of the course, and the chariots had to complete seven laps, about eight kilometres in all. Fouling was permitted, and collisions were frequent, especially at the turning posts (**metae**). A race began when the Emperor or presiding official gave the signal (**signum**) by dropping a white cloth (**mappa**).

The charioteers, some of whom won great popularity and very high salaries, were employed by four companies, each with its own colour—the "Reds" (**russati**), the "Whites" (**albati**), the "Greens" (**prasini**) and the "Blues" (**veneti**). Rival groups of spectators were accustomed to show their support (**favere**) for each colour vociferously.

One charioteer we hear about, Gaius Appuleius Diocles, drove chariots for the Red Stable for twenty-four years, ran 4257 starts and won 1462 victories.

MARCUS: Sexte! Sexte! hodie nobis licet ad ludos circenses ire. Eucleides me et te et Corneliam ad Circum ducet.

SEXTUS: ludos circenses amo. sed nonne Circus clausus erit?

MARCUS: minime! Circus non erit clausus, nam hodie cives omnes feriati sunt. viae erunt plenae hominum. viri, mulieres, liberi Circum celerrime petent.

SEXTUS: sed cur non nunc discedimus? ego sum iam paratus.

(But afternoon it had to be—and later than expected, for much to the boys' disgust Cornelia was rather late in waking up from her siesta.)

EUCLEIDES: agite! iam tandem ad Circum ire tempus est. estisne parati, pueri? esne parata, Cornelia?
(Eucleides takes Cornelia and the boys quickly through the streets; they can now hear the noise of the Circus crowds.)

EUCLEIDES: iam a Circo non procul absumus. nonne strepitum auditis? ecce! omnes ad Circum festinant. brevi tempore nos ipsi intrabimus.

(They enter the Circus.)

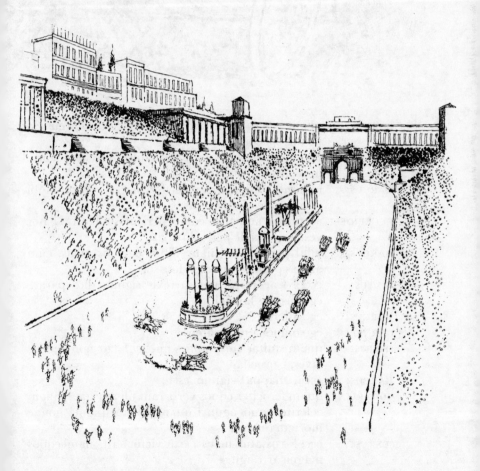

CORNELIA: quam ingens est turba hominum! totus Circus est plenus spectatorum.

EUCLEIDES: ita vero! semper multi spectatores in Circo sunt. hic considemus?

MARCUS: minime! prope arenam sedere necesse est quod ibi omnia videre poterimus.

EUCLEIDES: at prope arenam sedere periculosum est. pater vester multa de periculo dixit.

MARCUS: nihil periculi est, nam Titus, patruus meus, cum amicis prope arenam sedere solet.

SEXTUS: ecce! Caesar ipse iam surrexit; signum dare parat. ego russatis favebo.

MARCUS: ego albatis.

CORNELIA: ego omnes aurigas amo!

SEXTUS: quam stultae sunt omnes puellae! cur non venetis faves, Cornelia?

MARCUS: ecce! mappa! signum est!

CORNELIA: quam ferociter equos verberant illi aurigae! quam celeriter equos agunt! quam temerarii sunt! nonne mortem timent?

SEXTUS: ecce! russatus meus certe victor erit, nam equos magna arte agit.

MARCUS: o me miserum! auriga meus equos devertit. cave metam! cave metam! esne semisomnus, fatue? cur metam non vitavisti?

CORNELIA: eheu! ille auriga cecidit. in arena iacet. estne mortuus?

SEXTUS: minime! minime! ecce! animum recuperavit. iam surgit.

CORNELIA: audivistisne clamores horum spectatorum? magna voce nomina aurigarum et equorum semper clamant! undique ingens est strepitus! tantum strepitum ego numquam audivi.

MARCUS: russati hanc victoriam habent, sed mox etiam albati habebunt victoriam. gloria albatorum erit immortalis.

EUCLEIDES: hoc fortasse accidet, sed Caligula ipse, ut dicunt, prasinos amabat.

(*They watch a few more races, but it is not Marcus' lucky day. Eucleides becomes a little anxious as it grows darker. He had been caught once before in a crush at the gates.*)

EUCLEIDES: iam sero est. nunc domum redibimus; advesperascit enim. agite!

SEXTUS: nondum tempus est domum redire. ecce! aurigae habenas sumpserunt et signum exspectant.

PREFIXES I

Compare the following sentences:

1 equi raedam **trahunt**.	1 equi raedam **extrahunt**.
The horses **pull** *the coach*.	*The horses* **pull out** *the coach*.
2 servi lectum **ferebant**.	2 servi lectum **referebant**.
The slaves **were carrying** *the bed*.	*The slaves* **were carrying back** *the bed*.

In the second column something has been added to the beginning of the verb to alter its meaning or give it a more specific meaning. This additional part is called a *prefix*. Common prefixes are:

a-, ab-, abs-, away, from
ad-, towards, to
ante-, before
con-, along with, together
(or simply to emphasise)
de-, down, down from
di-, dis-, away, in different
directions
e-, ex-, out, out of

in-, into, in, on
inter-, between
per-, through (or simply
to emphasise)
prae-, in front, ahead
praeter-, past, beyond
pro-, prod-, forward
re-, red-, back, again
tra-, trans-, across

Note that many of these are common prepositions.

Exercise P1

1 *Give the meaning of:*
   (*a*) abire, adire, praeterire, transire, redire, exire, inire, praeire.
   (*b*) referre, transferre, adferre, conferre, inferre, praeferre.
   (*c*) discedere, excedere, incedere, recedere, procedere, antecedere, praecedere.
   cedo, cedere (3), **cessi, cessum,** to come, go

2 *Translate:*
   (*a*) pater liberos ex atrio eduxit et trans aream traduxit.
   (*b*) Cornelius Eucleidem iussit liberos abducere.
   (*c*) Eucleides liberos ad hortum reduxit.
   (*d*) servi togas et tunicas in cistis reponunt.
   (*e*) ubi ad Portam Capenam veniunt, servi onera deponunt.
   (*f*) ubi plaustrum invenit, stercus removit et corpus extraxit.
   (*g*) Cornelii Romam heri advenerunt.
   (*h*) homo per viam it. mox viam transibit et ad villam redibit.

PREFIXES II

Some prefixes undergo a change (often for ease of pronunciation) when they are added to verbs which begin with certain consonants:

(a) **ad-** The **d** tends to change to the consonant that follows it, e.g.

> accurro (from ad-curro)
> affero (from ad-fero)
> attuli (from ad-tuli)
> allatum (from ad-latum)

(b) **in-** and **con-** The same kind of change can take place with **in** and **con** before certain consonants, e.g.

> immitto (from in-mitto)
> irruo (from in-ruo)
> illatum (from in-latum)
> committo (from con-mitto)

Note that **in-** and **con-** become **im-** and **com-** before **b** or **p,** e.g.

> impono (from in-pono)
> compello (from con-pello)

(c) **ex-** becomes **ef-** in front of verbs beginning with **f,** e.g.
> effero (from ex-fero)

(d) **ab-** becomes **au-** in front of verbs beginning with **f,** e.g.
> aufugio (from ab-fugio)
> aufero (from ab-fero)

Exercise P2

Translate:

1 Geta effugere non potest.
2 caupo Corneliam et matrem ad cubiculum adduxit.
3 servi cistas in raeda imponunt.
4 servi onera ingentia in villam apportabant.
5 cibum ex villa aufert.
6 Aurelia in cubiculum Marci subito irrumpit.
7 Cornelia librum e manibus Sexti celeriter abstulit et in hortum aufugit.

> **rumpo, rumpere** (3), **rupi, ruptum,** to burst

PREFIXES III

Sometimes the verb undergoes a change when a prefix is added, e.g.

f**a**cere, *to make*	ref**i**cere, *to remake, repair*
t**e**nere, *to hold*	cont**i**nere, *to hold together, contain*
r**a**pere, *to seize*	arr**i**pere, *to seize towards oneself, snatch*
c**a**pere, *to take*	inc**i**pere, *to take on, begin*
cl**au**dere, *to shut*	incl**u**dere, *to shut in*

Exercise P3

Translate:

1 servi raedam reficiebant.
2 Sextus ad terram decidit.
3 subito Sextus librum arripuit et retinuit.
4 Cornelia ad villam redibit.
5 dominus servos a cubiculo excludit.
6 Aurelia servos togas in cistis reponere et domum referre iubet.
7 pueros, quod praecurrebant, identidem revocabat Cornelius.

ADDITIONAL EXERCISES

A. *Translate into English:*

brevi tempore ad villam ibimus. ibi ex atrio in hortum curremus; in horto cum amicis nostris ambulabimus; sub arboribus aestate sedebimus; septima hora cenabimus. vilicus Cornelii, nomine Davus, alios servos iubebit diligenter laborare; nonnumquam eos baculo verberat. decem diebus nos ad urbem redibimus.

B. *Translate into English:*

CORNELIA: quid heri fecisti, Marce? te invenire non potui.

MARCUS: postquam surrexi, ego et Sextus exire constituimus. ubi in vias ivimus, milites multos vidimus. miles quidam qui nos conspexit "unde vos venistis?" rogavit. "nonne pater vos iussit domi manere? pater tuus, ubi vos domi non invenit, me in urbem misit. me iussit vos domum statim ducere."

CORNELIA: quid dixisti? nonne militem timuisti?

MARCUS: ubi haec audivi, tacui, nam in vias exire non licuit. non militem timui, sed patrem. ego domum redire volui, sed Sextus "cur venisti, ignave," inquit "si patrem times? ego nolo redire" et in viam se praecipitavit.

CORNELIA: quid accidit?

MARCUS: miles eum petivit, togam arripuit. brevi tempore nos ad patrem duxit. Sextus effugere non potuit.

CORNELIA: punivitne vos pater?

MARCUS: non est necesse id rogare. sedere non possum.

C. *Translate into English:*

Cornelius in vias urbis descendit. in animo habebat aliquid liberis et uxori emere. ubi domum rediit, stolam novam Aureliae, Tito fratri statuam parvulam, Eucleidi librum versuum, duos mures Corneliae, clientibus suis pecuniam dedit. et Marco et Sexto? nihil! sed pueris "cras" inquit "vos ad Circum Maximum ducam et omnia vobis explicabo."

D. *Translate into English:*

Flavia Corneliae "salve!" scribit. "quando epistolam ad me scribes? tu promisisti sed nondum epistolam misisti. iam tibi omnia de villa nostra narrabo. patruus meus in villa iam manet, sed mox ad urbem veniet. fortasse parentes me cum patruo Romam mittent. tum poterimus cum matre tua tabernas visitare et novas stolas emere. scribe ad me! valde gaudebo si de urbe a te audiam."

E. *Translate into English:*

1 ego epistolam scribebam, tu in horto sedebas.
2 cras mane pater tuus me et te ad amphitheatrum ducet.
3 vos mox visitabo, sed in vestra villa non pernoctabo.
4 nos omnia de aedificiis urbis scimus, vos nihil scitis.
5 nonne mater tua tibi multa de nobis dixit?
6 dic mihi! quo heri ivisti? te non vidi.
7 tu nos semper accusas, sed nos nihil mali fecimus.
8 hodie mane uxor mea ad urbem mecum iter faciet.
9 tune voces servorum nocte audivisti? nos dormire non poteramus.
10 quid pater liberorum vos de eis rogaverat?

F. *Translate into English:*

1 hic puer in hac via, ille puer in illa via habitat.
2 illa puella in hac villa habitat; hi pueri in illa villa habitant.
3 nonne illud aedificium mox ad terram cadet?
4 si illud baculum conicies, hi canes ferociter latrabunt.
5 illi praedones illos viatores sub his arboribus petunt.
6 quando illi servi haec onera in aream villae portabunt?
7 noli illud plaustrum in hanc urbem interdiu agere!
8 huic puero multa dabimus, illi nihil.
9 his rusticis licebit agros huius villae colere.
10 huic senatori ad Curiam in lectica redire necesse erat.
11 illi aedificio appropinquare periculosum est, nam muri sunt infirmi.
12 unus ex his praedonibus aliquid illi servo dicebat.

G. *Translate, paying particular attention to the tenses of the verbs:*

vir quidam praeclarus, nomine Ulixes, ab urbe Troia redibat et uxorem suam Penelopam videre volebat. diu tamen ei non licebat domum redire, nam Neptunus, deus maris, iratus constituerat eum punire quod Ulixes filio Neptuni nocuerat. huc illuc igitur per multa maria errabat Ulixes, multas insulas visitabat, multa et mira animalia videbat. identidem deus eum in mare praecipitabat, identidem Ulixes incolumis effugiebat.

ubi ad insulam quandam venit, servavit eum dea quae ibi habitabat. cibum et vestes dedit; virum diu curabat; mox eum amabat et uxor eius esse volebat. sed Ulixes de uxore sua cogitabat. solus saepe lacrimabat neque volebat in illa insula manere. dea, ubi eum lacrimantem conspexit, "cur doles?" inquit. Ulixes "de Penelopa cogitabam" respondit. "quamquam me bene curas et multa mihi das, tamen domum redire volo."

tandem dea servos iussit navem, cibum, vestes parare, nam noluit eum retinere invitum.

deus, -i (*m*), god	**vestis, -is** (*f*), garment
mare, maris (*n*), sea	**navis, -is** (*f*), ship
insula, -ae (*f*), island	

Vocabulary

a, ab (+ *abl.*)	by, from
abeo, abire, abii, abitum	to go away
abhinc	ago, previously
absum, abesse, afui	to be away, be distant
accidit, accidere (3), **accidit**	to happen
accuso (1)	to accuse
ad (+ *acc.*)	to, at, near
adhuc	still
adiuvo, adiuvare (1), **adiuvi,** adiutum	to help
admoveo, admovere (2), admovi, admotum	to move towards
advenio, advenire (4), adveni, adventum	to reach, arrive at
advesperascit, -ascere (3), advesperavit	evening is coming on, it is getting dark
aedificium, -i (*n*)	building
aedifico (1)	to build
aestate	in summer
aestus, -us (*m*)	heat
affero, afferre, attuli, allatum	to carry towards
age! agite!	come on!
ager, agri (*m*)	field
ago, agere (3), **egi, actum**	to do, drive
quid agis?	How are you?
albatus, -a, -um	white
aliquid	something
alius, alia, aliud	other, another
alter, altera, alterum	the other, the second
ambulo (1)	to walk
amicus, -i (*m*)	friend
amo (1)	to like, love
amphitheatrum, -i (*n*)	amphitheatre
ancilla, -ae (*f*)	servant-girl
animal, animalis (*n*)	animal
animus, -i (*m*)	mind
animum recuperare	to regain one's senses
in animo habere	to intend
antea	previously, before
antiquus, -a, -um	ancient

76

aperio, aperire (4), **aperui, apertum**   to open
appareo (2)   to appear
appropinquo (1) (+ *dat.*)   to approach, draw near (to)
aqua, -ae (*f*)   water
aquaeductus, -us (*m*)   aqueduct
arbor, arboris (*f*)   tree
arcus, -us (*m*)   arch
area, -ae (*f*)   yard, courtyard
arena, -ae (*f*)   arena, sand
arripio, arripere (3), **arripui, arreptum**   to snatch, seize
ascendo, ascendere (3), **ascendi, ascensum**   to climb up, go up
Asia, -ae (*f*)   Asia Minor
at   but
atque   and also
atrium, -i (*n*)   atrium, central room in a house
attente   attentively, closely
attonitus, -a, -um   astonished, astounded
audio (4)   to hear, listen to
aureus, -a, -um   golden
auriga, -ae (*m*)   charioteer
aurum, -i (*n*)   gold
auxilium, -i (*n*)   help

B **baculum, -i** (*n*)   stick
bene   well
bona, bonorum (*n.pl*)   goods, possessions
bonus, -a, -um   good
bos, bovis (*m/f*)   ox, cow
brevis, brevis, breve   short

C **cado, cadere** (3), **cecidi, casum**   to fall
canis, canis (*m/f*)   dog
captivus, -i (*m*)   prisoner
caput, capitis (*n*)   head
cauda, -ae (*f*)   tail
caupo, cauponis (*m*)   innkeeper
caupona, -ae (*f*)   inn
causa, -ae (*f*)   reason
caveo, cavere (2), **cavi, cautum**   to watch out, be careful
celeriter   quickly
celerrime   very quickly
celo (1)   to hide

cena, -ae (*f*)	dinner
ceno (1)	to dine
certe	certainly
cesso (1)	to delay, loiter
cibus, -i (*m*)	food
Circus, -i (*m*)	Circus Maximus (a stadium in Rome)
cista, -ae (*f*)	trunk, box, chest
civis, civis (*m*)	citizen
clamo (1)	to shout
clamor, clamoris (*m*)	a shout, shouting
claudo, claudere (3), **clausi, clausum**	to shut
clausus, -a, -um	shut, closed
cliens, clientis (*m*)	client, hanger-on
cogito (1)	to think
colo, colere (3), **colui, cultum**	to cultivate
commotus, -a, -um	moved
ira commotus	angry, in a rage
metu commotus	frightened
conduco, conducere (3), **conduxi, conductum**	to hire
conicio, conicere (3), **conieci, coniectum**	to throw
consido, considere (3), **consedi, consessum**	to sit down
conspicio, conspicere (3), **conspexi, conspectum**	to catch sight of
constituo, constituere (3), **constitui, constitutum**	to decide
corpus, corporis (*n*)	body
cras	tomorrow
cubiculum, -i (*n*)	bedroom
cubitum ire	to go to bed
cum (+ *abl.*)	with
cum	when
cuncti, -ae, -a	all
cur?	why?
Curia, -ae (*f*)	Senate-house
curo (1)	to look after
curro, currere (3), **cucurri, cursum**	to run
custodio (4)	to guard
custos, custodis (*m*)	guard
D **de** (+ *abl.*)	down from, concerning
dea, -ae (*f*)	goddess

decem	ten
defessus, -a, -um	tired
deinde	then, next
demonstro (1)	to show
descendo, descendere (3), **descendi, descensum**	to go down, climb down
deus, -i (*m*)	god
devoro (1)	to devour
dico, dicere (3), **dixi, dictum**	to say, tell
dies, diei (*m*)	day
diligenter	carefully
discedo, discedere (3), **discessi, discessum**	to go away
diu	for a long time
do, dare (1), **dedi, datum**	to give
doceo, docere (2), **docui, doctum**	to teach
doleo (2)	to be sorry
domi	at home
domina, -ae (*f*)	mistress
dominus, -i (*m*)	master, owner
domum	home(wards)
domus, -us (*f*)	house
dormio (4)	to sleep
duco, ducere (3), **duxi, ductum**	to lead, take
dum	while
duo, duae, duo	two

E

e, ex (+ *abl.*)	from, out of
ecce!	look! look at!
effugio, effugere (3), **effugi**	to escape, run away
ego	I
eheu!	alas!
eius	his, her
emo, emere (3), **emi, emptum**	to buy
enim	for
eo	there, to that place
eo, ire, ivi, itum	to go
epistola, -ae (*f*)	letter
equus, -i (*m*)	horse
eram	I was
erro (1)	to wander
esse	to be
esto!	all right!
esurio (4)	to be hungry
et	and
etiam	also, even

euge!	hurray!
eugepae!	well done! hurray!
excipio, excipere (3), **excepi, exceptum**	to welcome, receive
excitatus, -a, -um	wakened
excito (1)	to waken
exclamo (1)	to exclaim, shout out
exeo, exire, exii, exitum	to go out
explico (1)	to explain
exspecto (1)	to wait for
exstans, exstantis	standing out, towering
extendo, extendere (3), **extendi, extentum**	to hold out
extra (+ *acc.*)	outside
extraho, extrahere (3), **extraxi, extractum**	to drag out

F

fabula, -ae (*f*)	story
facio, facere (3), **feci, factum**	to make, do
faveo, favere (2), **favi, fautum** (+ *dat.*)	to favour, support
feles, felis (*f*)	cat
feriae, -arum (*f.pl*)	holidays
feriatus, -a, -um	on holiday
fero, ferre, tuli, latum	to carry, bring
ferociter	fiercely
festino (1)	to hurry
filia, -ae (*f*)	daughter
filius, -i (*m*)	son
finio (4)	to finish
fortasse	perhaps
fortunatus, -a, -um	lucky
forum, -i (*n*)	the Forum (town centre of Rome)
fossa, -ae (*f*)	ditch
frater, fratris (*m*)	brother
frustra	in vain
fugio, fugere (3), **fugi, fugitum**	to flee
fui	I have been (perfect of **esse**)

G

gaudeo (2)	to rejoice
gaudium, -i (*n*)	joy
gemo, gemere (3), **gemui, gemitum**	to groan
gladius, -i (*m*)	sword
gloria, -ae (*f*)	fame, glory

Graecia, -ae (*f*)	Greece
Graecus, -a, -um	Greek

H
habenae, -arum (*f.pl*)	reins
habeo (2)	to have, hold
habito (1)	to live
haereo, haerere (2), **haesi,** **haesum**	to stick
heri	yesterday
hic, haec, hoc	this
hic (*adverb*)	here
hodie	today
homo, hominis (*m*)	man
homines, hominum (*m.pl*)	people
hora, -ae (*f*)	hour
hortus, -i (*m*)	garden
hospes, hospitis (*m*)	friend, guest
huc illuc	here and there
huic	dative of **hic**
huius	genitive of **hic**

I
iaceo (2)	to lie
iam	now, already
ianua, -ae (*f*)	door
ibi	there
idem, eadem, idem	the same
identidem	repeatedly
igitur	therefore
ignavus, -a, -um	lazy, cowardly
ille, illa, illud	that; he, she, it
illuc	thither, there
huc illuc	here and there
imber, imbris (*m*)	rain
immemor, immemoris	forgetful
immobilis, -is, -e	motionless
immortalis, -is, -e	immortal
in (+ *abl.*)	in, on
in (+ *acc.*)	into
incendo, incendere (3), **incendi, incensum**	to burn, set on fire
incito (1)	to spur on, urge on
induo, induere (3), **indui,** **indutum**	to put on
infirmus, -a, -um	weak, shaky
ingens, ingentis	huge
inquit	(he/she) says, said
inspicio, inspicere (3), **inspexi, inspectum**	to examine

insula, -ae (*f*)	island, tenement
interdiu	during the day, by day
interea	meanwhile
interpello (1)	to interrupt
intra (+ *acc.*)	inside
intro (1)	to enter
invenio, invenire (4), **inveni, inventum**	to find, come upon
invitus, -a, -um	unwilling, unwillingly
ipse, ipsa, ipsum	-self
iratus, -a, -um	angry
ire	see **eo**
is, ea, id	he, she, it; that
ita	in this way
ita vero!	yes
Italia, -ae (*f*)	Italy
itaque	and so, therefore
iter, itineris (*n*)	journey, road
iterum	again, a second time
iubeo, iubere (2), **iussi, iussum**	to order, bid

L **labor, laboris** (*m*)	work, toil
laboro (1)	to work
lacrimo (1)	to weep, cry
laetus, -a, -um	happy, glad
lapis, lapidis (*m*)	stone
latrans, latrantis	barking
latratus, -us (*m*)	barking
latro (1)	to bark
laudo (1)	to praise
lavo, lavare (1), **lavi, lavatum**	to wash
lectica, -ae (*f*)	litter
lecticarius, -i (*m*)	litter-bearer
lectus, -i (*m*)	bed, couch
legatus, -i (*m*)	envoy
lego, legere (3), **legi, lectum**	to read
lente	slowly
liber, libri (*m*)	book
liberi, -orum (*m.pl*)	children
licet (2)	it is allowed
longus, -a, -um	long
ludi, -orum (*m.pl*)	games
lutum, -i (*n*)	mud
lux, lucis (*f*)	light
prima luce	at dawn

M   **magnificus, -a, -um**   magnificent
    magnus, -a, -um   large, great, loud (of voice)
    mandatum, -i (*n*)   instruction
    mane   in the morning, early
    maneo, manere (2), **mansi,**
      mansum   to remain, stay
    manus, -us (*f*)   hand
    mappa, -ae (*f*)   napkin
    mare, maris (*n*)   sea
    mater, matris (*f*)   mother
    maximus, -a, -um   great, greatest, very large
    me   me
    medius, -a, -um   mid-, middle of
    Megara, -ae (*f*)   Megara (a city in Greece)
    mehercule!   By Hercules!, My goodness!
    melior, melioris   better
    mercator, mercatoris (*m*)   merchant
    meta, -ae (*f*)   mark, goal, turning-post (in
                             Circus)
    metus, -us (*m*)   fear
    meus, -a, -um   my, mine
    mihi   to me, for me
    miles, militis (*m*)   soldier
    minime!   not at all, not in the least, no!
    mirus, -a, -um   wonderful, strange
    miser, misera, miserum   unhappy, wretched
      o me miserum!   poor me! O dear me!
    mitto, mittere (3), **misi,**
      missum   to send
    modo   only
    moles, molis (*f*)   mass, huge bulk
    molestus, -a, -um   troublesome, annoying
    mons, montis (*m*)   mountain, hill
    monstro (1)   to show
    mors, mortis (*f*)   death
    mortuus, -a, -um   dead
    moveo, movere (2), **movi,**
      motum   to move
    mox   soon, presently
    mulier, mulieris (*f*)   woman
    multi, -ae, -a   many
    multitudo, multitudinis (*f*)   crowd
    murus, -i (*m*)   wall
    mus, muris (*m*)   mouse
    musso (1)   to murmur, mutter

N   **nam**   for
    narratus, -a, -um   told

narro (1)	to tell (a story)
navis, navis (*f*)	ship
-ne	(indicates a question)
necesse	necessary
neco (1)	to kill
nemo	no one
neque	and ... not
neque ... neque ...	neither ... nor
nihil	nothing
nihil mali!	no harm done!
nisi	unless, if ... not
nobis	to us, for us
noceo (2) (+ *dat.*)	to harm
nocte	by night
nocturnus, -a, -um	happening during the night
noli!	do not ... !
nolo, nolle, nolui	to be unwilling, refuse
nomen, nominis (*n*)	name
non	not
nondum	not yet
nonne?	(indicates a question)
nonnumquam	sometimes
nos	we, us
noster, nostra, nostrum	our
novus, -a, -um	new
nox, noctis (*f*)	night
nullus, -a, -um	no, none
numquam	never
nunc	now

O

obdormio (4)	to fall asleep
obesus, -a, -um	fat
occurro, -currere (3), **-curri, -cursum** (+ *dat.*)	to meet
oculus, -i (*m*)	eye
olim	once upon a time
omnis, -is, -e	every, all
onus, oneris (*n*)	burden, load
oppressus, -a, -um	crushed
optimus, -a, -um	best, very good
orator, oratoris (*m*)	orator, speaker

P

Palatinus, -a, -um	belonging to the Palatine Hill
paratus, -a, -um	prepared, ready
parens, parentis (*m/f*)	parent
paro (1)	to prepare

pars, partis (*f*)	part
parvulus, -a, -um	small, little
pater, patris (*m*)	father
patronus, -i (*m*)	patron
patruus, -i (*m*)	uncle
paulisper	for a short time
pecunia, -ae (*f*)	money
per (+ *acc.*)	through, along
periculosus, -a, -um	dangerous
periculum, -i (*n*)	danger
pernocto (1)	to spend the night
perterritus, -a, -um	terrified
pervenio, pervenire (4), **perveni, perventum**	to arrive at, reach
pes, pedis (*m*)	foot
peto, petere (3), **petivi, petitum**	to seek, aim at, make for, ask
plaustrum, -i (*n*)	wagon, cart
plenus, -a, -um	full
pluit (3)	it rains
poeta, -ae (*m*)	poet
pono, ponere (3), **posui, positum**	to place, put
pons, pontis (*m*)	bridge
porta, -ae (*f*)	gate
porto (1)	to carry
possum, posse, potui	to be able
post (+ *acc.*)	after
postis, postis (*m*)	door-post
postquam	after
postridie	on the next day
(se) praecipitare	to rush
praeclarus, -a, -um	famous
praecurro, praecurrere (3), **praecucurri, praecursum**	to run ahead
praedo, praedonis (*m*)	robber
prasinus, -a, -um	green
prima luce	at dawn
primum	first
princeps, principis (*m*)	emperor
procul	far, far off
promitto, promittere (3), **promisi, promissum**	to promise
prope (+ *acc.*)	near
puella, -ae (*f*)	girl
puer, pueri (*m*)	boy
punio (4)	to punish
purus, -a, -um	spotless, clean

Q

quadratus, -a, -um	squared
qualis?	of what kind?
quam!	how!
quamquam	although
quando?	when?
qui, quae, quod	who, which
quidam, quaedam, quoddam	a, a certain
quies, quietis (*f*)	rest
quiesco, quiescere (3), quievi, quietum	to rest
quis? quid?	who? what?
quo?	whither? where (to)?
quod	because
quod	see **qui, quae, quod**
quomodo?	how?
quoque	also

R

raeda, -ae (*f*)	coach, carriage
raedarius, -i (*m*)	coachman, driver
raro	seldom
redeo, redire, redii, reditum	to return, go back
reditus, -us (*m*)	return
relinquo, relinquere (3), reliqui, relictum	to leave
removeo, removere (2), removi, remotum	to remove, move aside
reprehendo, -hendere (3), -hendi, -hensum	to scold, blame
res, rei (*f*)	thing
rem explicare	to explain the situation
respondeo, respondere (2), respondi, responsum	to reply
revoco (1)	to call back
rideo, ridere (2), risi, risum	to smile, laugh
rimosus, -a, -um	full of cracks, leaky
risus, -us (*m*)	smile, laugh
rogo (1)	to ask
Roma, -ae (*f*)	Rome
Romanus, -a, -um	Roman
russatus, -a, -um	red
rusticus, -i (*m*)	peasant

S

saepe	often
saluto (1)	to greet, welcome
salve! salvete!	greetings! welcome!
satis	enough

scelestus, -a, -um	wicked
scio, scire (4), **scivi, scitum**	to know
scribo, scribere (3), **scripsi, scriptum**	to write
se	himself, herself, itself, themselves
sed	but
sedeo, sedere (2), **sedi, sessum**	to sit
semisomnus, -a, -um	half-asleep
semper	always
senator, senatoris (*m*)	senator
senatus, -us (*m*)	senate
septem	seven
septimus, -a, -um	seventh
sepulcrum, -i (*n*)	tomb
sequens, sequentis	following
sero	late
servo (1)	to save
servus, -i (*m*)	slave
sex	six
si	if
sibi	to himself, themselves
signum, -i (*n*)	signal
silentium, -i (*n*)	silence
simul	at the same time
simulac	as soon as
sine (+ *abl.*)	without
soleo (2)	to be accustomed, in the habit of
sollicitus, -a, -um	worried
solus, -a, -um	alone
somnium, -i (*n*)	dream
somnus, -i (*m*)	sleep
sonitus, -us (*m*)	sound
sordidus, -a, -um	dirty
spectator, spectatoris (*m*)	spectator
specto (1)	to look at
spina, -ae (*f*)	backbone
statim	immediately
statua, -ae (*f*)	statue
stercus, stercoris (*n*)	dung
sterto, stertere (3), **stertui**	to snore
stilus, -i (*m*)	pen
sto, stare (1), **steti, statum**	to stand
strepitus, -us (*m*)	noise, clattering
stringo, stringere (3), **strinxi, strictum**	to draw

gladium stringere	to draw a sword
stultus, -a, -um	stupid, foolish
stupeo (2)	to be amazed, gape
sub (+ *abl.*)	under, beneath
subito	suddenly
sumo, sumere (3), **sumpsi, sumptum**	to take, pick up
supra (*adverb*)	above, on top
supra (+ *acc.*)	above
surgo, surgere (3), **surrexi, surrectum**	to rise
suus, -a, -um	his, her, its, their (own)

T

tabellarius, -i (*m*)	courier
taberna, -ae (*f*)	shop
taceo (2)	to be silent
talis, -is, -e	like this, of this kind
tamen	however, nevertheless
tandem	at last, at length
tantum	only
tantus, -a, -um	so great, such a big
temerarius, -a, -um	rash, reckless, bold
tempus, temporis (*n*)	time
teneo (2)	to hold
terra, -ae (*f*)	earth, ground
terror, terroris (*m*)	terror, fear
tibi	to you, for you
timeo (2)	to fear, be afraid
timidus, -a, -um	afraid
toga, -ae (*f*)	toga
totus, -a, -um	all, the whole
trado, tradere (3), **tradidi, traditum**	to hand over
traho, trahere (3), **traxi, tractum**	to drag, pull
transeo, transire, transii, transitum	to cross
tremo, tremere (3), **tremui**	to tremble
tres, tres, tria	three
Troia, -ae (*f*)	Troy
tu	you
tuli	I brought (see **fero**)
tum	then, at that time
tumultus, -us (*m*)	commotion
turba, -ae (*f*)	crowd, mob